Young Children Reading

Young Children Reading

At home and at school

Rachael Levy

Los Angeles | London | New Delhi
Singapore | Washington DC

SAGE Publications Ltd
1 Oliver's Yard
55 City Road
London EC1Y 1SP

SAGE Publications Inc.
2455 Teller Road
Thousand Oaks, California 91320

SAGE Publications India Pvt Ltd
B 1/I 1 Mohan Cooperative Industrial Area
Mathura Road
New Delhi 110 044

SAGE Publications Asia-Pacific Pte Ltd
33 Pekin Street #02-01
Far East Square
Singapore 048763

Library of Congress Control Number: 2010938739

British Library Cataloguing in Publication data

A catalogue record for this book is available from the British Library

ISBN 978-0-85702-990-4
ISBN 978-0-85702-991-1 (pbk)

Typeset by C&M Digitals (P) Ltd, Chennai, India
Printed in India at Replika Press Pvt Ltd
Printed on paper from sustainable resources

Dedication
This book is dedicated to Daniel and Ben, who taught me
so much about children and reading.

Series published in association with UKLA

The emphasis for all of the books is this series is on developing practical skills for teachers in literacy and language teaching, underpinned by accessibly presented theory and research. Dealing with topics of current and continuing interest, the books aim to inform all those concerned with the development of literacy: teachers, researchers and local authority professionals, as well as those involved in teacher education and continuing professional development.

Books in the series:

Phonics: Practice, research and policy Maureen Lewis and Sue Ellis (editors), 2006

Visual Approaches to Teaching Writing: Multimodal literacy 5-11 Eve Bearne and Helen Wolstencroft, 2007

Desirable Literacies: Approaches to Language and Literacy in the Early Years (Second Edition) Jackie Marsh and Elaine Hallett (editors), 2008

The United Kingdom Literacy Association (UKLA) is a registered charity, which has as its sole object the advancement of education in literacy at all levels and in all educational settings in the UK and overseas. Members include classroom teachers, teaching assistants, school literacy co-ordinators, LEA literacy consultants, teacher educators, researchers, inspectors, advisors, publishers and librarians.

UKLA provides a forum for discussion and debate through a wide range of international, national, regional and local conferences and publications. UKLA works with a range of government and non-governmental agencies on issues of national interest. The Association is also committed to the funding and dissemination of high-quality national and international research projects that include practitioner-researchers. This series of co-published titles with Sage Publications complements the range of in-house UKLA publications and provides a further opportunity to disseminate the high quality work of the association. In order to find out more about UKLA, including details about membership, visit: http://www.ukla.org

List of Contents

List of Tables and Figures

Tables

Figures

Acknowledgements

First and foremost, thanks go to the ESRC for funding the doctoral study behind this book and funding a post-doctoral fellowship which has allowed time and support for the creation of this publication.

Sincere thanks also go to the children, parents and staff at Oakfield Primary School for allowing me this privileged opportunity to work so closely with them.

Special thanks go to Professor Jackie Marsh for her comments on drafts of this book, as well as her sustained interest and enthusiasm for the work.

Many thanks also go to Dr Eve Bearne and Dr Linda Hargreaves, who supervised my PhD and helped to guide the project at the heart of this book.

Thanks also go to my colleagues at the School of Education, University of Sheffield, for their continual support and interest in the writing of this book.

Finally, I extend my gratitude to my family and friends who have shown unwavering support while I have been writing this book. I am especially grateful to my husband, Nicholas, for his encouragement and commitment to all aspects of my study and work.

All names of individuals and settings mentioned in the book have been changed.

About the Author

Rachael Levy B(Ed), M Phil, PhD, is a Lecturer in Early Years Education at the University of Sheffield. She is responsible for the teaching and supervision of Masters, Ed D and PhD students studying various aspects of early childhood education. Having worked as a primary school teacher in London and in Cambridge, Rachael first began researching young children's perceptions of reading through the context of an M Phil in Teaching and Teacher Education. Following this, Rachael received an ESRC Studentship which allowed her to continue her studies to doctoral level at the University of Cambridge.

In July 2008, Rachael was awarded the UKLA Post Graduate Research Prize for her doctoral thesis. Rachael was also awarded an ESRC Post Doctoral Fellowship in the same year, which she completed at the School of Education, University of Sheffield. In addition to this book, Rachael has also published her work in a number of peer-reviewed journals and she has contributed chapters to other books in the field. As well as her interests in literacy and reading education, Rachael is also concerned about developing ways in which to access the voices of young children in participatory research.

Introduction

Learning to read is generally regarded as a crucial component of early years education. In fact the term 'starting school' is often seen to be almost synonymous with the term 'learning to read'. Teachers, parents and policy makers care about reading, and with good reason. As Byrnes and Wasik (2009: 171) point out, 'there is a direct and strong connection between reading skills and the level of academic and professional success enjoyed by an individual in his or her lifetime'.

Yet the teaching of reading has remained a contentious topic over the years, and has been fiercely debated in terms of approach. While much of the research in the field has sought to explore certain strategies and understand 'what works best' (McGuinness, 2005) in terms of reading instruction, in order to draw conclusions from this work we must be clear about our definitions of terms such as 'reading' and 'being a reader'. In other words, what do we mean when we say that a child is 'a reader' or has 'reading skills'? More specifically, to what extent are we implying a need for children to gain phonetic knowledge and develop the ability to decode printed text, or are we more concerned with children's broader interactions with texts and the abstraction of meaning (Arizpe and Styles, 2003; Martinez et al., 2003)?

There was a time when it was perceived that these perspectives on reading were in direct opposition to one another – hence the term 'reading wars' (Stanovich and Stanovich, 1999) became coined to describe the debate (though in reality few educationalists ever argued for complete reliance on either perspective). Nevertheless, it is clear that considerable disagreement has penetrated discussion on reading instruction over the years. However, it has recently been documented that a consensus view of reading does indeed exist that combines emphasis on meaning and understanding with phonetic knowledge (Snow et al., 1998). This consensual view came about when a group of 17 experts on reading stated their combined agreement that reading can be defined as 'a process of getting meaning from print, using knowledge about the written alphabet and about the sound structure of oral language for purposes of achieving understanding' (1998: vi). Snow et al. go on to assert that 'skilled readers' are therefore able to combine their knowledge of letters and sounds with broader meaning-making strategies (such as general world knowledge) in order to make sense of spoken language and text, as well as developing 'text-specific' processes to comprehend texts.

Yet this definition appears to assume that there is universal agreement on what is meant by the term 'text'. Much of this work is grounded in the assumption that 'texts' are paper based and largely pertain to the handling of books. However, it is apparent that the texts children read in modern society extend beyond those of paper-based media and include the 'new textual landscapes' (Carrington, 2005: 13) of popular culture, digital and screen media. Advances in computer technology in particular have prompted a considerable shift in the ways in which children read texts today. As Bearne et al. point out, 'reading habits are changing as reading increasingly involves the use of electronic sources and new technologies. The reading skills required for accessing information are also changing' (2007: 2).

This has huge implications for young children entering the formal schooling system today. For example, we can no longer assume that books are the dominant medium that children will be using to access information in their homes and within their broader communities. In the UK, Marsh et al. (2005) conducted a wide-scale study of 1,852 parents of children aged from birth to 6 years, in order to investigate young children's use of popular culture, media and new technologies. They concluded that their data painted a picture of early childhood in the twenty-first century as 'technologically-mediated, littered with popular cultural icons and shaped by the fashions and passions of media' (Marsh et al., 2005: 47). Moreover, they further reported that the young children in their study were often 'technologically astute and digitally competent' (2005: 47) but that their exposure to technology such as computers and game consoles was still balanced with time spent outdoors, playing with toys and reading books and being read to.

This presents quite a challenge for teachers, policy makers and researchers working in early years education, as the discourse on reading and reading education has clearly entered a new phase. Reading is no longer just about reading books, but neither is it about just reading digital texts. Rather, children entering the formal education system today are immersed in a variety of reading practices that include the reading of paper texts (books, comics, magazines and so on) together with the reading of digital and screen texts. This places new and complex demands on young readers which are, as yet, poorly understood. In order to develop this understanding, this book therefore takes a broad and inclusive view of reading that acknowledges this complexity faced by young children as they learn how to read within the modern society in which they live.

Though research on reading has provided a valuable insight into many aspects of reading development, much of this work has failed to acknowledge the impact of digital technology on the ways in which children make sense of texts today. Yet if we, as educators, are to support young children in becoming confident users of texts within the twenty-first century, it seems imperative that we gain a deeper understanding of the strategies that are used and indeed required in order to read the variety of texts in existence today. Given the multimodal nature of modern text, it has been argued that the descriptors of reading development in the literacy curriculum must be reviewed in order to reflect 'the skills and strategies which children bring to their understanding of screen texts' (Bearne et al., 2007: 29). Yet it must be further recognised that print reading is still regarded as 'the primary form of communication' (Hall, 2003: 173) within society and therefore within schools. For this reason, the role that print decoding plays in the reading of multimodal texts seems especially important if we are to develop an understanding of the complex nature of children's reading today.

One of the major aims of this book is therefore to explore the ways in which print reading fits within the broader constructions of reading that are generated by young children's exposure to multimodal texts. Though the use of phonics instruction to teach reading has remained a controversial subject over the years, research (see Adams, 1990, for a review of empirical research in the field) suggests that 'children who are taught about the alphabet and letter – sound correspondences go on to be better readers and spellers (Stainthorp, 2003: 217). However, it is also widely accepted that becoming a successful reader involves the development of many key skills and 'involvement in many social processes' (Beard, 2003: 206). Given that the landscape of literacy and communicative practices is changing so rapidly, and that the 'social processes' connected with multimodal text use are not fully understood, it does seem to be of particular importance that we learn how print literacy functions within this new discourse on reading, and that we develop strategies to teach print literacy that are appropriate to this changing discourse.

But how can we do this? This brings us right back to the question of definition. If we want to learn how factors such as print literacy influence the ways in which children interact with texts today then we need to understand how young children perceive the process of learning to read. This involves an understanding of how young children come to define the terms 'reading' and 'being a reader' during their early years in school. Moreover, we also need to understand how certain factors influence the development of these definitions, and the implications of this for children's confidence in themselves as readers.

This book explores these issues through the context of case study research that was conducted with twelve young children at the time of entry into the formal education system. This study, referred to as 'The Oakfield Study', employed a range of techniques to collect data directly from children who were in Nursery (aged 3–4 years) and Reception (aged 4–5 years) at the beginning of the project. The children were followed over the course of one complete academic year and data were collected in three distinct phases. The purpose of the study was to understand the nature of the children's perceptions of themselves as readers as they began formal schooling, and to acknowledge changes that occurred as the children became more emerged within the school discourse. Data were collected within the children's homes and in school, to help understand the influence of home and school discourse on the children's perceptions of reading and subsequent perceptions of themselves as readers.

Findings from this study are used throughout this book to structure discussion and explore the issues raised above. Given that very little previous research in reading has attempted to understand the perspectives of young children, this book aims to provide all those concerned with reading in the early years, including teachers, researchers and policy makers, with the insight needed to improve the teaching of reading within the Foundation Stage and beyond. By maintaining a focus on the voices of the children themselves, this book demonstrates how young children draw from the discourses operating at home and at school, to develop their own perceptions of what reading is, and formulate beliefs about what it means to be a reader today. On the basis of this understanding, this book also presents the implications this has for teachers and practitioners working within early years settings.

Structure of the book

This book has been structured so that each chapter builds on previous chapters. Therefore, it is recommended that chapters are read in the sequence they are presented in order for the reader to benefit from this continuity. However, it is appreciated that certain chapters may be of particular interest to some; for example, those wishing to focus on the use of reading schemes may find that Chapter 4 is of most interest.

Each chapter ends with a Summary, including Key questions which invite reflection on classroom practice. In addition, Chapter 7 focuses specifically on the ways in which practitioners can reflect on, and modify their practice in order to address the issues raised in this book. It is intended that the Key questions will help students and practitioners to focus on particular aspects of classroom practice and make applications between theory and practice. These questions have also been included to help those involved in the professional education of teachers. Teacher trainers can use these questions as part of structured activity, or to promote discussion in the classroom in relation to the teaching of reading within early years settings.

Overview of the book

The opening chapter provides a foundation for the rest of the book in that it firstly presents an outline of the various ways in which 'reading' has been defined in the literature. Using the work of Kathy Hall (2003) as a guide, this chapter discusses four perspectives on reading that have been identified in the literature and their relevance towards the teaching and learning of reading in schools today. In particular, these perspectives are examined in the light of 'the digital age', with an emphasis on the ways in which developments in digital technology have influenced and changed the landscape of reading practice. Having discussed these various perspectives on reading, the chapter then turns to the research which has shaped this book. The second half of the chapter therefore presents an overview of the case study research (The Oakfield Study) which was designed to gain an understanding of young children's perspectives on reading and perceptions of themselves as readers. A detailed account of the research design is presented, including the research methods employed and the tools and techniques created and used to collect the data from the children. As parents and teachers were also interviewed during this study, these interview schedules are also described. The chapter also provides a brief account of the ways in which profiles were developed for each child in the study so that conclusions could be drawn on the basis of this data.

All the children in The Oakfield Study are introduced to the reader in Chapters 2 and 3. The main purpose of these chapters is to present an outline of the children's individual definitions of reading and the factors that influenced the formation of these definitions. Chapter 2 focuses on the Nursery cohort and demonstrates how these children were drawing from their own home experiences in developing ideas and beliefs about what reading is and what it means to be 'a reader'. These children presented definitions of reading that were far broader and more holistic than the Reception children, whose definitions were considerably narrower. The Reception children's definitions of reading, presented in Chapter 3, suggested that these children were less likely to see themselves as 'readers' because they did not believe they had the skills to match the definition of reading which they believed operated within school. This chapter concludes with a discussion based upon the perceptions of children from both cohorts, and reflects on the ways in which factors inherent within a child's definition of reading can influence both how children tackle text and how they develop confidence in themselves as readers.

Building on this, Chapter 4 focuses on book texts and their perceived role within the process of learning to read. Given that the children in The Oakfield Study reported that reading scheme texts were crucial in both defining what is meant by the term 'reading' and in dictating how children learn to read, these texts are discussed in detail. In particular, this chapter examines the ways in which reading scheme texts are linked to issues of proficiency grading and self-confidence in reading. Serious concerns are raised about using reading schemes in the Foundation Stage and about allowing them to dominate young children's perceptions of themselves as readers. Given that this raises particular issues for teachers working in early years settings, implications for practice are discussed in the Summary of this chapter as well as the final chapter of the book.

Chapter 5 shifts the focus from book texts to the reading of multidimensional and multimodal texts. This chapter discusses how children may develop a range of strategies to make sense of texts through their engagement with digital and screen texts in their homes. These strategies include the handling of print alongside the decoding of other sign and symbol systems which are inherent within multimodal texts. However, this chapter also demonstrates how many of these skills can become lost as children encounter more formalised constructions of reading within Reception. As a consequence, this chapter discusses the ways in which early years practitioners can build on the skills children acquire within their home settings and help young children to become confident users of a wide range of texts, including those of paper and screen contexts.

The role of the home environment is discussed further in Chapter 6, which explores how home and school discourses on reading can promote continuities and discontinuities for young children as they journey through their early years in school. This chapter draws on the concept of 'third space theory' to critically reflect on the ways in which young children's perceptions of reading are influenced by their transition into the school setting. By reflecting back on the data already described in this book, this chapter demonstrates how the space in between the discourses of home and school can cause disruption for some children as they struggle to reconcile their experiences of reading within their home settings with the expectations of the school system.

The implications of this for the teaching and learning of reading within early years is discussed explicitly in Chapter 7. This chapter invites practitioners to reflect critically on aspects of their practice and evaluate the ways in which reading instruction may influence children's confidence in themselves as readers and have an impact on motivations for reading. The chapter maintains a focus on the role of the practitioner and particularly those working within the Foundation Stage of the curriculum. Teachers are asked to consider how their own perceptions of reading can influence the ways in which they present reading education to their children. Moreover, teachers are invited to reflect critically on the ways in which they personally develop relationships with children and the learning environment and to recognise how even subtle changes in practice can help young children to develop the skills and confidence to become effective readers of text in the twenty-first century.

The concluding chapter turns to the question of policy and provides suggestions for change on the basis of issues raised in this book. In particular, this chapter makes specific recommendations for change within the Foundation Curriculum, in order to provide teachers with more opportunities to teach reading within a holistic environment that is free from the constraints of proficiency grading. Implications for future research are also discussed in this chapter.

This book does not pretend to be a guidebook or instruction manual, telling teachers how to teach reading. Rather, it exposes the complex nature of reading in modern society and urges all those involved in the education of young children to recognise this complexity and adapt their practice to meet the needs of young children growing up in a digital world. On the basis of sound research findings, this book provides researchers and practitioners with the insight required to develop strategies to meet the challenges of the twenty-first century, and to support young children in becoming confident and motivated readers of text from their earliest years in school.

1

Becoming a reader in a digital age

Chapter Overview

Issues surrounding the teaching of reading are complex. Part of this complexity arises from the fact that definitions of the terms 'reading' and 'being a reader' are becoming increasingly open to debate. As highlighted in the Introduction, children's exposure to texts are changing in the light of developing technologies and advancements in multimedia and with this change comes a demand for readers to learn how to employ a variety of reading skills in order to access both paper and screen-based texts. However, if these skills are not recognised within the school system, then the issue does indeed become one of contention. If teachers are to help young children develop confidence in themselves as readers, then there is much to gain from understanding how young children are making sense of the terms 'reading' and 'being a reader' themselves. In particular it is important that early years educators recognise how the settings of home and school influence the ways in which young children come to define reading and the impact this has upon their confidence in themselves as readers and their motivations to read. These issues are examined in detail in the chapters to follow. The purpose of this chapter is therefore to provide a foundation for this discussion. To begin, the chapter presents a brief reflection on the different ways in which definitions of reading have been perceived and documented in the literature. This provides a useful backdrop for the rest of the book which invites the children's voices into the debate. This is largely achieved through reference to a case study that was conducted with twelve children who were in their early years of schooling. As this study has played a pivotal role in the formation of this book, this chapter also describes how the research was developed. In particular, given that the research was specifically designed to access the voices of these young children, this chapter explains how various play-centred techniques were developed and implemented in order to acquire reliable and valid data from these young children.

Definitions of 'reading'

This following section explores some of the theoretical perspectives within the field of reading education which offer definitions of the terms 'reading' and 'being a reader'. Though many definitions are in existence, for reasons of clarity these have been classified under four broad headings using the work of Hall (2003) to structure the discussion. In her insightful publication *Listening to Stephen Read: Multiple perspectives on literacy*, Hall invites the reader to consider a variety of perspectives on reading through direct consultation with well-known reading scholars. While it must be stressed that these perspectives rarely operate in isolation from one another, a point emphasised by Hall herself, and that many teachers and early years professionals have drawn implicitly and eclectically from them over the years, these perspectives allow us to reflect on some of the specific ways in which young children may be influenced by the discourse on reading.

The cognitive-psychological perspective

This perspective on reading relates to the somewhat traditional phonetic approach, whereby children are taught to decode words by building an awareness of the segmental structure of language. This emphasis on the systematic teaching of word recognition and response to print is described as 'the hallmark of a cognitive-psychological perspective' on the teaching and learning of reading' (Hall, 2003: 77).

One particular assumption behind this approach is that children learn how to read in stages. For example, Gough and Hillinger (1980) argue that the first stage is one of 'paired-associate learning', where children initially begin to associate spoken words with particularly salient visual clues, often within their local environment. For this reason Gough and Hillinger maintain that this stage often involves the reading of environmental print. Stanovich and Stanovich (1999: 21) argue that this is a 'natural' stage. However, they go on to claim that 'normal progress in reading dictates that the child makes the transition to the next stage of acquisition, which requires some degree of visual and speech analysis'. They stress, however, that this stage is not 'natural' and argue that some degree of intervention is almost always required from an outsider.

This intervention is associated with the structured teaching of phonics. Many researchers argue that children need to be able to tackle words using their phonetic knowledge, especially when faced with unfamiliar words or when contextual clues fail to be of use (Nicholson, 1993; Gough and Hillinger 1980; Stanovich, 1980). It has also been argued that children who are reading 'well' by the age of 6 are those who have developed phonological recoding processes (Stuart et al., 1999). The structured teaching of phonics currently occupies a substantial component of the Primary National Strategy[1], especially within Key Stage 1. The government document *Progression in Phonics* (DfES, 1998) was used widely in schools as a means of teaching young children phonetic knowledge before being adapted (*Playing with Sounds,* DfES, 2004) to 'take account of more recent research on the pace and sequence of phonic teaching' (UKLA, 2006: 3.21). Both documents have now been replaced with a new scheme entitled *Letters and Sounds* (DfES, 2007).

Given that such national strategies for the teaching of literacy encourage teachers to employ a range of techniques to promote reading at the level of the letter, word, sentence and whole text, structured phonetic knowledge has generally been taught alongside other skills to acquire meaning from texts. Indeed the United Kingdom Literacy Association (UKLA) recommends that 'the existing pace of phonics teaching … is retained' (2006: 3.23). However, there is substantial concern that the government's recommendation to base early reading instruction on synthetic phonics[2] (Rose, 2006) is inappropriate and unjustified by research.

Firstly, it has been documented by the US National Reading Panel (NRP) that while 'specific systematic phonic programs are all significantly more effective than non-phonic programs … they do not appear to differ significantly from each other in their effectiveness' (National Institute

---

[1]The Primary National Strategy (2003) was developed to build upon the Literacy and Numeracy strategies, placing them in a wider whole-school framework.

[2]Synthetic Phonics programmes emphasise the conversion of letters (graphemes) into sounds (phonemes) and then blending sounds to form words. This differs from Analytic Phonics programmes which introduce children to whole words before moving towards relevant phonic generalisations.

of Child Health and Human Development, 2000: 93). Subsequently, similar findings have also been reported within UK (Torgerson et al., 2006) and Australian (Australian Government Department of Education Science and Training, 2005) contexts. Secondly, the Rose Report (2006: 29) claims that it is 'highly worthwhile and appropriate to *begin* a systematic programme of phonic work by the age of five, if not before for some children'. While it has now been reported that the government will not proceed with the proposed curriculum, based upon the Rose Review, it is clear that the suggestion raised serious, justified and on-going concerns amongst early years educators (Wyse and Styles, 2007). Wyse and Styles argue that it is highly inappropriate to impose such a curriculum on young children, especially given the fact that 'the majority of evidence in favour of systematic phonics teaching refers to children age 6 and older' (2007: 37). Finally, there is concern that the context within which the Rose Report suggests phonics teaching should be implemented contradicts much previous evidence generated from research in reading over the last few decades. In particular the approach has been criticised for being 'over-prescriptive' (UKLA, 2006: 9.1) and disconnected from whole text work (Wyse and Styles, 2007).

The psycho-linguistic perspective

Much of the writing on the psycho-linguistic perspective on learning to read is derived from the belief that 'all language is used for authentic purposes' (Hall, 2003: 41). This commitment to 'authenticity' resulted in one particular movement in the teaching of reading, known as the 'real book approach' (Waterland, 1985). In brief this involved the use of 'real books' in the teaching of reading, rather than using structured reading scheme material.

Yet as highlighted by Campbell (1992: 1), the term 'real books' relates not just to the actual books children are given to read, but to 'the methods to be used and ... the teaching and learning environment to be provided'. In other words, the real book approach is a philosophy of teaching and learning that centres on the book, child, teacher and the whole interaction with the book, to ensure that the task is meaningful for the child. With specific reference to the Australian context, Turbill describes 'the age of reading as meaning-making' as the time in which readers were seen to 'bring meaning to print' as well as 'take meaning from print' (2002: 4). In the USA, Goodman (1986) defined a similar philosophy to the teaching and learning of reading as the 'whole-language' approach, where again the focus was on understanding the meaning of language as a whole, rather than on simply decoding the minutiae of print.

This approach has also been described as a 'top-down conceptualization' (Smith, 1971). This largely means placing emphasis on the contextual clues within a text, encouraging the reader to make full use of syntactic and semantic information available. Stanovich and Stanovich (1999: 14) point out that this strategy, whereby children are encouraged to guess at words based on the context of a previous passage, is still regarded as an 'efficacious way of reading and of learning to read' by many advocates of 'whole-language' approaches today. Yet, as exemplified in the work of Waterland (1985), this approach to the teaching of reading was never divorced, by most advocates, from the teaching of phonics or whole-word recognition skills.

However, both of the approaches so far discussed fail to acknowledge the complexity of issues surrounding the ways in which children learn to read and become readers of a variety of different texts. The next two sections examine some of the broader perspectives on reading which look beyond the 'primacy of mind' (Hall, 2003: 134) and recognise that learning to read is a complex process, rooted in social, cultural and political practice.

The socio-political perspective

The socio-political perspective regards literacy as being 'embedded within discourses of power' (Hall, 2003: 153). This notion of literacy as a powerful discourse has been raised by many; for example, Crowther et al.'s (2001) *Powerful Literacies* aims to promote literacy as a potent tool for challenging existing inequalities and dependencies. Similarly, Luke and Freebody (1999–2000: 4) also postulate that the social practice of literacy is 'necessarily tied up with political, cultural and social power and capital', and stress the importance of context within the construction of meaning in texts.

Certainly schools appear to have much power in determining what is meant by terms such as 'literacy' and 'reading'. Indeed, studies have demonstrated, for example, that many parents feel insecure about the ways in which they can support their young children in literacy development, as they fear they are not using 'correct' methods of instruction (Hannon and James, 1990; Oritz and Stile, 1996). Yet it must be recognised that schools themselves are governed by the requirements of a curriculum such as that set out in the National Literacy Strategy. Many would agree with Hall that the emergence and rationale of this strategy, with the 'highly prescriptive nature of its content and pedagogy'

(2003: 189), makes it difficult for teachers to incorporate critical literacy practices into their delivery of the curriculum.

The ways in which children's and parents' views of literacy are influenced by governmental power is one aspect for consideration within a socio-political perspective on reading. But to return to Hall's definition of this perspective, she argues that this connection between literacy and power is also related to the ability to 'determine underlying assumptions and hidden biases in texts' (2003: 176). Jones also refers to the power within texts in his elaborate portrayal of the reader–writer–text relationship. He argues that reading is a highly complex process, through which the reader is actively involved in a cycle of interpretation and response. Rather than such 'response' being necessarily reflective, he argues that the term 'points to the pragmatic force of reading [and] its power to prompt changes of thought or action' (1990: 163).

Hall argues that this approach to reading means that one 'sees literacy not as neutral but as bound up with ethnicity, gender, social class, disability and so on' (2003: 189). While all of these issues are relevant to children's interactions with texts, the relationship between gender and reading has received particular attention from researchers. For example, the quest to understand gender differences in the schooling of literacy has been documented in publications such as Millard's (1997) *Differently Literate*. However, as others have pointed out, such debates have been criticised for being too simplistic in their binary positionings of gender (Weaver-Hightower, 2003; MacNaughton, 2000), with Millard herself now arguing that the debate needs to move towards 'more subtle and nuanced approaches' (2003: 29). In particular, many now agree that while gender does influence children's achievements in literacy, other factors, such as social class, have a far greater impact on attitude and attainment in literacy activity (Moss, 2007; Smith, 2003). This suggests that in order to understand children's engagement with reading, we must look towards the whole social and cultural context within which reading is seated.

The socio-cultural perspective

A socio-cultural perspective is defined as shifting emphasis from the individual to 'the social and cultural context in which literacy occurs' (Hall, 2003: 134). In other words, a socio-cultural perspective will not separate learning to read and write from the context in which it happens. This is vividly portrayed in the work of Heath (1983) whose ethnographic study of two communities in south-eastern USA revealed that children's language development is embedded in a deep cultural context and is profoundly influenced by the community discourse within which the child is immersed. Moreover, much further study has demonstrated the importance of a child's home environment upon all aspects of language acquisition (Tizard and Hughes, 1984; Compton-Lilly, 2006). For example, in her ethnographic study of three families, Pahl (2002) concluded that children's meaning making is a complex process, shaped by family structure and family narratives, while Minns (1997) raised awareness of the social and cultural influences upon children's early understanding of reading and writing in her study of five pre-school children.

Yet many have stressed their concern that children's home literacy practices are not valued within the school system. This issue has been explored in detail by Marsh (2003a; 2003b), who argues that a dissonance exists between 'out-of-school and schooled literacy practices' (2003b: 369). She states that children's out-of-school communicative practices need to be integrated into the school setting, having found 'more evidence of nursery practices infiltrating the home than visa versa' (2003b: 369). Marsh argues that recognition of the home literacy practices of young children is now a 'standard and routinely practised discourse' (2003b: 369), yet she makes the point that multimodal forms of meaning making experienced by children in their home settings do not penetrate early years educational settings. What is more, Marsh has also demonstrated the ways in which popular culture and media texts shape children's identities, yet she argues that further extensive analysis of children's multimodal text making and text responses in the home is needed so that early years educators can 'build on the extensive expertise that children already have as media consumers and users of new technologies' (2003b: 46).

Much of this work recognises that the ways in which children interact with texts in the home differs from 'schooled' constructs. This has been explored in detail in relation to children's interactions with visual texts and images (Kress, 2000; Arizpe and Styles, 2003; Walsh, 2003). Moreover, Anning challenges what she describes as 'the narrow versions of literacy' in schools, arguing that we:

> need to broaden our understanding of literacy to include young children's representations in graphic and narrative versions, influenced by the media and everyday exchanges with siblings and significant adults, that characterize their journeys towards literacy in home settings. (2003: 5)

Kress also forcibly asserts that young children's own representations need to be awarded greater recognition. He claims that children see the complexity 'of the meaningful cultural world with absolute clarity, and in their making of meaning they construct elaborate complex representations of the world' (1997: 97). Much of this work is urging schools to place greater value upon children's reading and indeed creation of visual and multimodal images during their early years. Yet as raised by Pahl, what is missing is a rigorous theoretical framework 'in which to set children's communicative practices, visual, textual and artefactual ... one that both attends to the way the home is structured and the cultural resources the home draws upon' (2002: 145).

Clearly more work needs to be focused on the role of children's 'out-of-school' literacy experiences if children's home literacy practices are to be valued appropriately in schools. However, Tudge et al.'s (2003) study of 20 pre-school children warns that such issues of value may be especially problematic for children from certain social groups. They concluded that middle-class pre-schoolers engaged in more 'school-relevant activities' (2003: 42–3) in the home than working-class children. Moreover, as these children were also reported to be more likely to initiate and engage in conversation, they 'were subsequently perceived by their teachers as being more competent'. Tudge et al. are here suggesting that children from middle-class families are more likely to present skills and abilities that are valued in the schooling system in comparison with children from working-class homes. In addition, this study goes on to suggest that children may have to learn to transfer their own representations of the world into a form that concurs more closely with the representations expected by a school environment in order to experience success within the school system.

This issue was also raised by Brooker (2002) who explored pre-schoolers' engagement with 'school-relevant activity' in relation to cultural privilege. Her book charts the fascinating journey of sixteen 4-year-old children – half of them from Bangladeshi families – as they began formal education. She discovered that many aspects of cultural background provided advantage for the 'Anglo' children and disadvantage for the Bangladeshi children, despite the 'good intentions' of teachers. Even though the children in Brooker's study were all from a poor inner-urban neighbourhood, she discovered that the Anglo children began school with a far greater understanding of what was expected from them in the school setting. Moreover, she concluded that the

Anglo children's home learning activities concurred more closely with that of the school's aims, compared with the Bangladeshi children.

Work such as this recognises not only the importance of the child's home practices in relation to literacy development, but also the impact of factors affecting transition from one setting into another. This relates to Bronfenbrenner's (1979) theory of the ecology of human development. Bronfenbrenner addresses the concept of transition as children transfer from one system into another, identifying the enormous complexities that face young children as they move within and across *microsystems*[3] and *mesosystems*[4]. Intrinsic to this is the child's ability, or attempt, to transfer knowledge from one system into another (such as from home into school). Yet one must recognise that the child is continually exposed to new rules or 'codes' (Bernstein, 1971) that govern how they should operate within certain systematic structures, such as the school environment.

This is a particularly salient issue for this book which is concerned with the ways in which children perceive reading at the time of entry into the formal education system. As emphasised in the above literature, children develop their own representations of literacy practice in the home before entry into the formal school environment. Yet it appears that children must not only learn the new 'codes' of a schooled discourse when they enter the school system, but must also find a way to cope with the impact of transition from one setting into another. This issue is explored in detail through the context of the case study data upon which this book is based. The study, which shall be referred to as 'The Oakfield Study', is now described. The next section explains how the study was designed so that the voices of the young children participating in the research could be accessed.

The study

Given the need to gain an in-depth understanding of young children's perceptions, this research used a case study approach, following two cohorts of children all from the same primary school. The first cohort were in Nursery (aged 3–4 years) when the study began, while the second group were in Reception (aged 4–5 years). Data were collected

---

[3]Bronfenbrenner (1979) describes this as 'a pattern of activities, roles and interpersonal relations experienced by the developing person in a given setting with particular physical and material characteristics'.

[4]This is the interconnection of two or more microsystems.

Table 1.1   Children's details

Name*	Class	Birthday	Place in family	First language
Malcolm	Reception	August	2nd of 2	English
Toby	Reception	November	1st of 2	English
Simona	Reception	February	1st of 2	Spanish
Imogen	Reception	October	2nd of 2	English
Annie	Reception	June	1st and only	English
Joseph	Reception	February	1st and only	English
Kelly	Nursery (morning)	December	1st of 2	English
David	Nursery (morning)	November	2nd of 2	English
Huda	Nursery (afternoon)	July	1st and only	Arabic/English
Caitlyn	Nursery (afternoon)	November	3rd of 3	English
Shaun	Nursery (morning)	September	2nd of 2	English
Ibrihim	Nursery (afternoon)	October	4th of 4	Bengali

*Pseudonyms have been used for reasons of confidentiality

over the course of one complete academic year, with the children being followed into a new year during the course of the study. As Table 1.1 illustrates, the sample contained equal numbers of boys and girls and some children for whom English is a second language. The children were also selected on the basis of age so that the sample included children whose birthdays spread throughout the year.

The school was selected partly on the basis of its multicultural and diverse social catchment. It has its own Nursery which is situated within the same building as the two Reception classes. Positioned close to the centre of the city, the school attracts children from a wide range of social, cultural and ethnic backgrounds. It is a large, popular school of 414 pupils, of whom a quarter travel from outside the catchment area. The 12 per cent of pupils known to be eligible for free school meals matches the national average. The number of pupils speaking English as a second language is high at 24 per cent. The number of children on the register of Special Educational Needs is below average at 17 per cent. In a recent OFSTED inspection, the teaching of pupils aged up to 5 years was assessed as 'very good', whereas teaching was reported to be 'good' within the rest of the school.

Ethical considerations

Using the BERA (2004) Ethical Guidelines as a guide, the ethical considerations described below were integrated into the project. Once the sample had been selected, a letter was sent to the parents of each child explaining the aims and structure of the study and stressing the longitudinal nature of the work. The parents all subsequently provided written consent for their children to participate in the study and to be interviewed themselves in their home environment.

In addition to receiving consent from the parents, it was also regarded as extremely important that consent should be obtained from the children. Yet given the age of the children, it was recognised that issues of informed consent could be problematic. France argues that in order to achieve informed consent from children, we must 'enter into a dialogue with them about the aims and objectives of the research and about our practice' (2004: 183). But it was clear that the children in this study (aged between 3 and 5 years) were really too young to be expected to comprehend the exact purposes of research such as this.

In their study of 5-year-old children, Nutbrown and Hannon (2003) provide an excellent example of ways in which consideration can be shown towards the ethical issue of informed consent from young children. Having secured parental permission in their study, interviewing protocols were drawn up so that all members of the interviewing team would offer a clear explanation to the children about the interview, ensuring that the children understood that they did not have to participate if they did not wish to. The researchers also stressed to the children that the interview could be stopped at any time. What is more, the interview schedule was piloted with a number of children, who were asked to comment on how they felt when being interviewed. This included being asked if they 'liked it' and if they 'minded' being interviewed.

Using these ideas as a guide, many steps were taken to ensure that the children were comfortable with the research situation. For example, time was built into the schedule for the researcher to get to know the children before the process of data collection began. The research activities themselves were all designed to be as much fun as possible for the children and allowed time for the children to play with any artefacts to be used in the research situation.

The research methods: designing the tools

Very little research into aspects of literacy development has attempted to include young children as research participants. In fact the younger the child the fewer attempts seem to have been made to access views directly (Nutbrown and Hannon, 2003). Yet it is becoming increasingly recognised that reliable consultation with young children is indeed possible, but new methods to facilitate their participation must be developed and more widely used (Cremin and Slatter, 2004). Speaking of research into various aspects of literacy in particular, Nutbrown and Hannon draw our attention to the fact that researchers over the years have tended to rely on observational methods in order to understand children's learning, and stress that 'far less attention has been given to listening to children and soliciting their views on matters of daily life and learning' (2003: 117–18).

For this reason, the activities selected for this study were all based around the concept of 'interview'. However, the use of traditional interview techniques was clearly inappropriate for children of this age. This point was raised by Kellett and Ding who stated that it has been common for:

> researchers to consider children below the age of seven or eight years as not viable as interviewees, partly because of their young age ... But many writers and professional associations are now challenging this notion, maintaining that poor data are not necessarily a product of the young age of the child but of inappropriate interview techniques. (2004: 167)

This study is grounded in the belief that young children are in no way inherently 'less reliable' as respondents than adults (Scott, 2000). Yet as Greig and Taylor (1999) point out, participatory research with young children is 'special' and does make specific demands upon research design in order to secure reliable and valid data. Therefore, one challenge for this study was to design interview-based tools that would facilitate the acquisition of valid and reliable data from children as young as 3 years old. Nutbrown and Hannon (2003: 118) have identified two specific concerns that researchers have raised in relation to the acquisition of valid and reliable data from very young children. They stressed firstly that researchers feared that children 'may give you the answers that they think you want' and secondly that children 'may not understand the question', even though Nutbrown and Hannon go on to stress that 'these are exactly the same concerns that need to be addressed when interviewing adults' (2003: 106).

Given these concerns, several steps were taken during the design of the research to ensure that the data acquired could indeed be defended. Firstly, it was recognised that a play-orientated structure would increase the face validity of the interview data, as this would be a familiar context for the children. Secondly, it has commonly been acknowledged that young children will often provide answers to questions even if they do not actually know the answer (Scott, 2000; Kellett and Ding, 2004), rather that provide a 'don't know' response. This specific issue was explored in a study by Waterman et al. (2001) who deliberately asked nonsensical questions to young children. They discovered that when children were offered a nonsensical closed question, a response was given, but when offered a nonsensical open question the children were more likely to say that they did not understand the question, or did not know the answer. With this in mind, this study attempted to structure activities around the use of open-ended questions wherever possible and care was taken to ensure that terminology used was familiar to the children. Finally, the role of the researcher was given particular consideration as discussed below.

The role of the researcher

One main issue for this study was the concern that the children could view the researcher as a teacher, as this could influence the responses of the children. As Kellett and Ding highlight, 'if a researcher's role becomes blurred with that of a teaching role children may expect more guidance and direction in their responses, and not be as forthcoming' (2004: 166). For this reason, a major challenge for the project was to create distance between the researcher and the actual process of data collection. This was largely achieved through the use of props. In particular the use of a glove puppet (Charlie Chick) was piloted and then used throughout all three phases of the main study. While the use of such props has been seen to encourage children's engagement and interest (Brenna, 1995) it also meant that the entire interview could be conducted through the medium of a 'third party'. As the children were told that Charlie Chick knew very little about school but really wanted to learn some things from the children, they were offered the role of 'expert' within the school context.

Figure 1.1   Small World Play

Another prop used to create distance in the study was Small World Play equipment (see Figure 1.1). Essentially a 'home scenario' was set up using a variety of play equipment such as home furniture and small character dolls. Again the use of the role-play situation allowed questions to be centred on the characters in the scenario, rather than on the children themselves. In further activities the children were asked to talk about other children appearing in pictures and photographs. These activities all helped to create distance between the researcher and the child. This subsequently helped to increase the validity of the data as potential expectations created by the child–researcher relationship itself were reduced.

Data collection

Data were collected during three phases as illustrated in Table 1.2. As the research was concerned with understanding changes in the children's perceptions, some activities were repeated throughout all three phases of the study so that comparisons could be drawn between phases. The activities were also designed in a way that allowed certain themes to be continually revisited both within phases and across phases. This was important for reasons of validity as it meant that findings could be defended as they were drawn from a whole variety of related data.

Table 1.2 Overview of data collection

Phase	Data collection	Year groups
1 Summer 2005 (May–July)	Children – Charlie Chick interview (school) Small World Play activity (school) Unstructured interview (home) Teachers – Interview Parents – Interview in home	Nursery and Reception
2 Spring 2006 (January–April)	Children – Charlie Chick interview (school) Small World Play – Computer- assisted activity (school) Observation (school) Teachers – Interview (new teacher)	Nursery ⟶ Reception Reception⟶ Year 1
3 Summer 2006 (May–July)	Children – Charlie Chick interview (school) Small World Play activity (school) Unstructured interview (home) Parents – Interview in home	Reception and Year 1

Research Activities

Most of the school-based data were collected through the context of
two main activities: the Charlie Chick interview and the Small World
Play research conversation. Over the course of the year, these broad
activities often included a variety of 'branch activities' which have been
called:

- Learning Skills

- 'Exit'

- Book and Screen

- Popular Culture

- Computer-assisted

- Smiley Face

- Home and School Reading

- Book-bag.

In addition to these activities, interviews were also conducted with the children and their parents in their homes during the first and third phases of the study. The children's teachers were also interviewed in the first and second phases. Although most of the activities were designed to invite responses directly from the children, observation techniques were also employed in the second phase of the research. This next section now provides a brief explanation of all the tools used to collect data in this study.

 ## Charlie Chick interview

Much of the data were collected through the context of school-based interviews, which used a glove puppet (Charlie Chick) to mediate a conversation between researcher and child. Having been told that Charlie Chick has 'a bad memory' and struggles to remember all that he is told, the children were asked if they minded having the session recorded to help Charlie Chick 'remember' what they had said. All of the children agreed to have the sessions recorded. Through the context of these interviews, the children were engaged in conversations with the puppet about many different aspects of reading. For example, Charlie Chick asked to have terms such as 'reading' and 'being a reader' explained. Moreover, through the context of these interviews the children were invited to *show* the puppet what reading is, as well as describe how they felt about the activity.

Small World Play research conversation

This activity took the form of role play, using Small World Play equipment including a family of dolls (mother, father, younger sister, younger brother and an older sister), lounge furniture (including chairs, television, video and table), study furniture (including a desk, chair, computer and printer) and bedroom furniture. This activity investigated the children's perceptions of screen and paper-based reading, particularly in relation to the home environment. Through the context of play, the children were encouraged to talk about the ways in which various character dolls would use certain texts (television, computer, books, etc). In particular the children were encouraged to talk about the younger siblings in the family, describing, for example, what they did when they came home from school and their attitude towards reading the books in their book-bag. Questions relating to the children's perceptions of gendered choices were also embedded into this aspect of the investigation.

These research conversations were also designed to investigate the children's specific perceptions of multidimensional text use in the home and perceptions of print reading within multidimensional forms. This involved, for example, placing the dolls in front of the television and the computer and asking the children to comment on the use of such media and the dolls' 'abilities' to use such equipment. The children's perceptions of the dolls' attitudes towards print within multimodal contexts were given particular attention.

As stated, these main research activities were supplemented with a variety of branch-activities. These were essentially a range of short games and activities each designed to investigate how the children perceived aspects of print reading within a variety of multimodal contexts. Table 1.3 demonstrates how these branch activities were built into the overall research design.

Table 1.3   Overview of school-based activities with children

Phase	Activity	Name	Method	Main aim	Branch activities included
Phase 1	1 (Part 1)	Charlie Chick Part 1	Interview	To explore understandings of terms 'easy' and 'hard'	Learning Skills
	1 (Part 2)	Charlie Chick Part 2	Interview	To explore perceptions of print literacy within different contexts	'Exit' Book and Screen (A) Popular Culture Computer-assisted
	2	Small World Play	Research conversation	To explore children's perceptions of reading in the home	
Phase 2	3	Charlie Chick	Interview	To explore changing perceptions of reading	Learning Skills Popular Culture Book and Screen (B)

(Continued)

Table 1.3   (Continued)

Phase	Activity	Name	Method	Main aim	Branch activities included
	4	Small World Play	Interview/ Observation	To explore perceptions and uses of multi-dimensional texts	Computer-assisted (*Sebastian Swan*) (*Bob the Builder*)
Phase 3	5	Charlie Chick	Interview	To consolidate perceptions of reading To explore perceptions of proficiency judgement	Smiley Face Home and School Reading Learning Skills

Activity: Learning Skills

Having already been asked some general questions by Charlie Chick about things that were 'easy' or 'hard' to do at home and at school, the Learning Skills activity was introduced to specifically explore the children's perceptions of reading in terms of difficulty in relation to other activities. This involved Charlie Chick 'showing' the children a set of photographs, each presenting a child (the same child) engaged in an activity. The children were told that the child in the picture was *learning* to perform the various skills demonstrated in Figure 1.2. The children were then asked to decide whether it was 'easy' or 'hard' to learn to do the activity, and to place the photograph in a corresponding pile. Some children chose to include a 'middle' pile when performing this activity, so they could choose from three groupings rather than just the two.

Skills shown in picture
Riding a bike
Reading a book
Running
Tying shoelaces
Reading words on a computer screen
Painting a picture
Writing words with a pencil
Writing words on a computer

Figure 1.2   Pictures of skills used in the Learning Skills activity

Activity: 'Exit'

The children were shown a variety of cards each containing the word 'exit' in various forms. This included a Fire Exit sign, a picture of a door with the word 'Exit' above, the 'main menu' page of a computer game displaying the options *Load game, Play, Exit* and a card with the word 'Exit' printed in plain font. The children were asked to talk about the pictures and explain how they knew what the print said in each case. This activity helped to understand how the children were responding to print in a variety of multimodal forms.

Activity: Book and Screen

This activity used a picture of a child reading a book and a second picture of a different child (but of the same gender) reading from a computer screen. Through the medium of Charlie Chick, the children were then asked a series of questions to investigate their perceptions of reading paper and screen-based texts. For example, they were asked questions such as, 'Which child is having the most fun?' and 'How does this child understand what is happening on the computer/in the book?'

Activity: Popular Culture

In this activity Charlie Chick introduced the children to two sets of cards. Set 1 displayed the names of a variety of popular culture characters (such as Scooby Doo) written in a plain font text. The corresponding set of cards (Set 2) also displayed the names of the popular culture characters but this time written in their iconic/logo form. The popular culture characters used in this activity are presented in Figure 1.3.

Popular Culture characters
Barney
Bob the Builder
Scooby Doo
Tweenies
CBeebies
Barbie
Thomas the Tank Engine

Figure 1.3   Popular Culture cards

(Continued)

(Continued)

The children were firstly given the cards from Set 1 and asked if they recognised anything on them. It was of course anticipated that many of the children, especially those in the Nursery cohort, would not identify the printed text. The children were then given the set of iconic cards and again asked if they recognised anything on these cards. Throughout this stage the children were also asked to explain how they knew what was written on the cards. Finally, through the context of a game with Charlie Chick, the children were asked to try and 'match' the two sets of cards. This helped to identify the strategies the children were using to make meaning from printed and iconic symbols.

Activity: Computer-assisted

The computer was used in the first and second phases of the study to further explore aspects of the children's interactions with screen texts and perceptions of print reading within this context. In the first phase of the study the children were initially shown a laptop computer and asked if they could show Charlie Chick what they could do with it. While this activity provided an opportunity to investigate the strategies each child used to make sense of computer texts, it was recognised that the extent to which each child was able to use the computer with independence would clearly depend on the individual child and previous experience in handling such texts. While the children were all offered a choice about how they used the computer during the activity, most chose to download a *Humpty Dumpty* game which appeared as an icon on the desktop. In order to play the game, the children had to create a nursery rhyme-type story by making selections from various options available. For example, having selected a character from a choice of six options, the children had to decide where the character was going to go for an adventure, what treasure would be found and so on. At each subsequent stage the children were offered a choice of about three options from which to make a selection. The game offered the children a range of visual and auditory clues in order to guide their progress.

In the second phase of the data collection, the children were encouraged to play some specified games on the computer. All of the children were given the games *Sebastian Swan* and *Bob the Builder*. However, in some cases the children also chose to download a further game from the internet which was familiar to them.

Computer Text 1: *Sebastian Swan*. This game featured a series of 'big books' resembling those found in an infant classroom. The children were simply encouraged to read the books from the screen in any way they chose and were observed doing so. As the game featured 'books' which were very similar to paper-based books, this activity provided an opportunity to examine whether the physical medium of the computer in any way encouraged the children to read the books differently from the ways in which they read paper-based books.

Computer Text 2: *Bob the Builder*. A series of four games were downloaded from the *Bob the Builder* website. Although it was recognised that *Bob the Builder* could in itself be regarded as a highly gendered facet of popular culture, the games all displayed features that were extremely useful for the purposes of this activity. Subsequently, analysis of this activity focused solely on understanding the strategies used by the children to access, use and make sense of the texts and not on the children's attitudes towards the subject content. Table 1.4 provides some information about the four games and the demands made upon the reader in each case.

Table 1.4   Using the Bob the Builder games

Name of game	Objective	Keyboard tools used	Moving image	Auditory cues	Examples of iconic symbols	Examples of print
Muck's Maze	To steer a truck through a maze	Arrow keys	Controlled by player	No	'Home' symbol, 'Muck's Maze' icon	Back, Start, Finish, Play again?, Yes, No
Slider puzzle	To reassemble a jumbled picture	Mouse	Controlled by player	No	'Home' symbol, 'Slider puzzle' icon	Show hints, easy, medium, difficult, back
Spud and Pickle	To play a game of 'noughts and crosses', but with characters	Mouse	Controlled by player	No	'Home' symbol, 'Spud and Pickle' icon, character icons	You win, You lose, Play again?, Select a level
Scrambler's Ramble	To race a truck and collect 'sunflowers'	Arrow keys	Yes	Yes	Truck, 'Home' symbol, 'Scrambler's Ramble' icon	Help, Play Back, Ready, Steady Go, number scores

(Continued)

(Continued)

Activity: Smiley Face

Issues related to the home and school reading of paper texts were further investigated during the Smiley Face activity. The children were presented with a series of photographs each illustrating an aspect of home or school paper-text reading. These activities are presented in Table 1.5. The children were then given a scale of 'faces' to represent how they felt about each activity (Figure 1.4) and were asked to choose a face to describe each picture. They were told that the pictures meant *I like it, I don't like or dislike it* (or *I don't mind it or I don't know*) and *I don't like it* respectively.

Table 1.5   Pictures used during the Smiley Face activity

School reading activity	Home reading activity
Guided reading	Reading schoolbook to parent/adult
Looking at Big Book on carpet	Looking at schoolbook alone
Quiet/individual reading time	Looking at own books alone at home
Reading to teacher/adult in school	Parent/adult sharing child's own books
Teacher reading to whole class	Parent/adult reading child a story
Reading words on wall/displays	Listening to audio book*

*Although an audio book is not a 'paper text' as such, it was included in this section as several of the children had previously spoken of listening to audio books – and many are indeed accompanied by a paper text.

Figure 1.4   Sliding scale of Smiley Faces

Activity: Home and School Reading

This final branch activity involved the children being given large pictures of a school and a home as well as a series of smaller pictures showing a computer and various paper texts. These props were used to initiate a discussion about the kinds of activities the children enjoyed and/or expected to do at home and at school and what they believed to be involved in performing these activities. The purpose of this activity was to identify any differences in perception according to setting.

Activity: Book-bag

This activity took place during the final Charlie Chick interview. The children were told that Charlie Chick had now begun Nursery and had brought his book-bag (containing a reading scheme book) in to show the children. This allowed for the children to talk about their perceptions of reading scheme books and the role they play in the process of 'learning to read'. As well as the reading scheme book, Charlie Chick also brought a picture book and a non-fiction book to show the children. Through the medium of the puppet, the children were then asked a series of questions designed to explore their thoughts on the affordances of books in general. For example, they were asked which of the books they thought their parents and teachers would want them to read and why.

Teacher and parent interviews

In addition to the activities so far described, home visits took place during the first and third phases of the study. As well as providing an opportunity to observe the child in their own home environment, it was also useful to see how the child interacted with people and artefacts within their own home environment. This also proved to be useful in drawing comparisons between home and school discourses.

As well as observing the child, questions were also asked of the parents within the context of a semi-structured interview. Examples of questions asked to parents are presented in Figure 1.5. Some questions were also asked directly to the children depending on individual circumstance and the interest of the child on the day.

Teachers were also interviewed during the first and second phases of the study (bearing in mind that the children would all have moved into a new class during the year of data collection). This interview was designed to fulfil two main aims. Firstly, it provided an opportunity to learn more about the general day-to-day running of the classroom and thus give context to the study. Secondly, these interviews contributed towards the development of the children's case profiles through the provision

Sample questions asked to parents
General What does your child like doing when s/he is at home? Does s/he have favourite toys/games/activities? *Specific* Does s/he like to watch television? Which programmes? Does the family have/use a computer? Does your child use it? What does s/he do on it? How would you describe your child's attitude to school life? What is your child's response to the process of learning to read? Does s/he enjoy using books?

Figure 1.5   Examples of questions asked to parents

Sample questions asked to teachers
General Can you tell me a little about the daily routine in the Nursery/class? What activities do the children particularly enjoy/find easy/find hard? *Child-specific* How would you describe her/his attitude towards school life? What does s/he particularly enjoy doing/dislike doing? Does s/he show an interest in learning to read? Does s/he elect to use the computer? What does s/he do on it?

Figure 1.6   Examples of questions asked to teachers

of background information from the perspectives of the teacher. Examples of questions asked to teachers are presented in Figure 1.6.

Developing the case studies

The activities described above deliberately 'overlapped' so that central themes were explored repeatedly within a variety of different contexts during the research. For example, Figure 1.7 demonstrates how the children's perceptions of reading computer texts were explored from a variety of different perspectives and within different contexts over the course of the year. What is more, certain activities such as *Learning Skills* were conducted at each stage of the data collection, so that specific findings could be traced and compared over the course of the year for each child in the study.

All of the interviews were transcribed and grouped together for each child in the study. This meant that by the end of the first phase, profiles could be drawn up for each child on the basis of four broad themes.

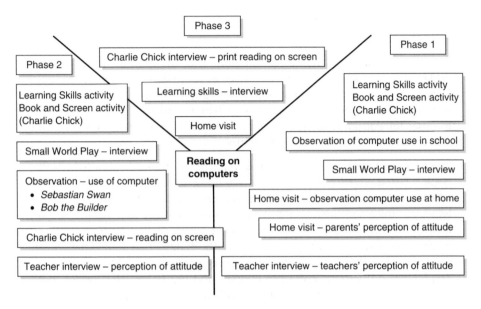

Figure 1.7   Example of thematic strand within data collection

These themes were: attitude towards school, perceptions of reading, reading on the computer and reading print in multidimensional forms. As the study progressed, these themes were broadened to also include specific reference to children's definitions of reading and being a reader, issues of attainment and enjoyment, print reading on screen and in books, and home and school constructions of reading. The profiles themselves underwent a further stage of analysis so that patterns and themes could be identified between the profiles as well as within the individual cases. This meant that conclusions were reached on the basis of findings drawn from a synthesis across the cases as well as an in-depth exploration of each individual journey over the course of the year.

☐ Summary

This chapter has looked at some of the ways in which the terms 'reading' and 'learning to read' have been defined in the literature. Using the work of Hall (2003) as a guide, various perspectives on reading have been discussed; these have included the decoding of print and the acquisition of meaning from

(Continued)

(Continued)

paper-based media, as well as an exploration of the broader social, cultural and political factors that influence children as they become readers in modern society. Given these issues, it has been further argued that definitions of reading must now include children's interactions with multimedia and digital technology in order for educators to help children to become competent and confident readers of text in the twenty-first century.

This chapter has also presented an account of the research upon which this book is based. This has included a detailed description of the research design which was created and implemented to access the voices of young children. Issues of ethical consideration and concern for reliability and validity of data have also been discussed within the context of this participatory research. By means of conclusion, it is hoped that the methods described in this chapter can be adapted by others wishing to access the voices of young children in research. The following questions invite practitioners and researchers to consider some salient factors in the design of research with young child respondents.

Key questions 🔑

- What research activities can I design in order to collect useful data from young children?
- How can I ensure that the activities will invite valid responses?
- Are the activities set within a meaningful context and do they reflect the age and experience of the respondents?
- Where is the researcher positioned within the research and how will this influence the quality of the data collected?
- Could the activities lead to misunderstandings between the conceptualisations of researcher and child?
- Are there any specific aspects of language or terminology that could cause ambiguity?
- What are the ethical implications of conducting this research?

2

Children's perceptions of reading: defining 'reading' in the Nursery

Chapter Overview

The previous chapter identified that there are a variety of different ways in which to perceive the term 'reading'. Yet there are certain factors that influence how we come to form definitions of reading and shape our beliefs about what we think reading actually is, and that is what this chapter focuses on. Consider for a moment how you would define the term 'playing the piano'. Would you consider this an appropriate term to apply to someone who is randomly striking the keys on a piano or does the term imply some greater degree of skill? If so, what must a person be able to do in order to be considered 'able' to play the piano? Should they be able to play a melody that is recognisable to others as a tune? Should they be able to read music and transfer this knowledge to their playing and if so, with what degree of accuracy? Should they be able to play by ear, improvise or compose? Or is the term defined by proficiency grading in the form of staged music examinations?

The answers to the questions raised above depend on a whole variety of factors, including the age of the person playing the piano, how long the person has been playing, any training received and the expectations of the player and the audience. This final point is particularly important. If an individual wishes to learn to play the piano purely for personal pleasure, then a definition of what it means to be 'able to play' could differ significantly from that assigned to a person wishing to pass graded music examinations. Similarly,

(Continued)

(Continued)

definitions of what 'reading' means will vary according to the age and experience of the reader. However, unlike learning to play the piano, it is expected that all children will learn to read during their early years in school. As a result, this expectation has an influence on how the term is perceived and defined.

When one takes into consideration the socio-political perspective on reading, as discussed in the previous chapter, we are reminded that definitions of the term are likely to be highly influenced by the curriculum and formal policies on the teaching and assessment of reading in schools. But what does this mean for young children as they enter the schooling system? To what extent are their experiences of reading within their home environments compatible with the discourse operating in school? Are there tensions between the two which cause disruption for some children during their earliest years in school?

These questions underline the importance of gaining insight into the perspectives of children themselves. Without access to the children's voices, it is simply not possible to understand how the merging discourses of home and school influence the ways in which young children develop confidence and motivations to read. Chapter 1 presented an outline of the study guiding this book, including a description of the activities conducted in order to collect data directly from young children. On the basis of findings from this study (The Oakfield Study), the next two chapters now examine how children's definitions of reading are shaped by experiences at home and at school and the implications this can have in terms of developing perceptions of the self as a reader. As highlighted, this case study followed the journeys of two separate cohorts of children: one beginning in the Nursery (aged 3–4 years), the other in Reception (aged 4–5 years). As a result, the first phase of the study was the only phase in which data were gathered from Nursery-aged children. This data proved to be especially valuable in illuminating the ways in which young children develop ideas and beliefs about reading, as these Nursery-aged children had less exposure to the school discourse on reading in comparison with those in the older cohort. This chapter now introduces each of the children from the Nursery cohort and explains how they came to develop individual definitions and understandings about reading. The following chapter then looks at the definitions of reading reported by the Reception children. This chapter is then concluded with a critical reflection on the ways in which children from both cohorts came to develop perceptions of reading and the implications this has for the schooling of reading in early years.

The Nursery cohort

Findings from this study revealed that the children in Nursery had far broader constructions of reading in comparison with the Reception children. Out of the Nursery sample, Shaun, Huda and Ibrihim provided responses suggesting that they all saw themselves as readers, yet their perceptions of what it meant to be 'a reader' differed significantly.

Profiles: Shaun, Huda and Ibrihim

Shaun – aged 4 years 10 months (September birthday)[1]
First language – English
Ethnic origin – Anglo/African
Place in family – second of two (father also has two older children who live with his first wife)

Shaun is a quiet yet confident boy, who lives with his mother, father and six-year-old sister. Shaun's mother and father both work but their working week is structured so that responsibility for child care is shared between them. Shaun is an articulate child who readily engages in conversations with adults and children. Classroom observations suggest that Shaun is keen to participate in all elements of activity in the Nursery and is well liked by adults and other children. Shaun's teacher described him as an 'able' and 'sociable' child. His mother described him as 'a thinker', reporting that he shows interest in a variety of different activities, including imaginative play, interactive games, reading and writing.

Huda – aged 3 years, 11 months (July birthday)
First language – Arabic/English
Ethnic origin – Arabic/British
Place in family – first and only

Huda's father is Arabic and her mother is English. Huda's mother reported that she and her husband are keen to foster Huda's Arabic identity, so Huda attends an Arabic Saturday school and regularly visits family in Syria. The family also subscribe to Arabic channels on Satellite television which constitute most of the family's television viewing. Huda speaks Arabic and English with fluency. She is an articulate and sociable child who appears to be well liked by adults and other children. She seems to enjoy all aspects of Nursery life and readily engages in a wide variety of play-based activities. She especially enjoys playing with dolls and owns a substantial collection of Barbie dolls, including an Arabic Barbie.

---

[1]Ages documented in this section can be taken as age of child at the beginning of the study.

(Continued)

(Continued)

Ibrihim – aged 4 years 8 months (October birthday)
First language – Bengali (also fluent in English)
Ethnic origin – Bangladeshi
Place in family – fourth of four

Ibrihim lives with his mother, father and three siblings. He has an elder brother and sister who are in their teens as well as a six-year-old sister. Ibrihim's father works as a taxi driver while his mother remains at home caring for the children and home. There is a large extended family, many of whom live close by. Ibrihim is particularly close to his grandmother (his mother's mother) who he sees regularly. Ibrihim's teacher reported that Ibrihim can play independently for long periods of time, though he also integrates well with his peers. He has a passion for jigsaw puzzles, with his teacher reporting that he can sustain concentration on puzzles, 'all afternoon'. Ibrihim's teacher also described him as being very 'alert' and 'with it', reporting that he regularly asks questions when at school.

Perceptions of being 'a reader' in Nursery

Shaun was described as being the most interested in letters and phonics, with his teacher reporting that 'he's *really* interested in letters and things', and his parents agreeing that he is 'very keen' (mother) to learn to read, and is 'very inquisitive' (father) about the whole process. Shaun's mother also reported that Shaun is 'very much paying attention' when his six-year-old sister is reading her schoolbook at night and enjoys trying to 'guess what the word is' if his sister 'goes wrong'.

Yet despite the fact that Shaun was already developing advanced print-decoding strategies for a child of his age, this was not necessarily what made Shaun 'a reader' in his own eyes. Although he did report that 'reading is when you look at letters and you read it' he also reported that reading was 'easy', simply because he was 'big' enough to do it. Having also claimed that Charlie Chick would be able to read soon when he too was 'big', he went on to argue that his two-year-old cousin could not read because 'he is little' but stated that 'when it's his birthday he will be able to read'. In other words, Shaun appeared to believe that reading is an attainable skill for anyone who is *old enough* to be able to read. Similarly, Huda also appeared to believe that reading can be easily achieved by anyone who is old enough. For example, when asked what it means if someone cannot read, she replied that a non-reader is 'a little baby', but went on to report that 'mummies and daddies' and 'big girls' can read. Like Shaun, she too reported that she thought Charlie Chick was able to read because he was not 'a baby'.

Although Huda and Shaun both believed that anyone can read once they are 'big', they also both reported definitions of reading that related to the deconstruction of text. For example, despite his interest in the decoding of print, Shaun acknowledged that he used a variety of strategies to make meaning from texts, reporting that everything on the page including 'the words' and the pictures, 'is part of the story'. In fact, even though Shaun was able to decode some aspects of printed text, he was very reluctant to suggest that these skills were more important than picture-reading skills and argued that we 'needed both' print and pictures in books. Having focused on the pictures in a book when showing Charlie Chick what reading is, Shaun then reported that he knew what the story was about 'because the front has got dinosaurs on ... and this bit has got dinosaurs on [pointing to the illustrations]'. Furthermore, when Charlie Chick pointed to the title and asked what it is, Shaun suggested that it could say *'Charlie and the Dinosaurs'*. This illustrates that Shaun was not just demonstrating an awareness of what print is, but was using the pictures and the context of the story to make a sensible guess as to what the print could reasonably say. It therefore appeared that Shaun owned a very holistic definition of reading that included the use of pictures, print and context.

For Huda, reading books appeared to be synonymous with simply enjoying them. Having consistently reported that she could read and that she liked reading books, even though she was not yet print literate, she spontaneously offered to show Charlie Chick what reading was. Huda then selected a book and became instantly absorbed in the pictures, grinning and laughing at the characters and making comments such as, 'Look at that!' or 'The duck says "Quack quack"'. Yet further comments suggested that Huda may have been beginning to realise that something more structured could be expected from a definition of reading, beyond issues of enjoyment. For example, Huda found it initially very difficult to answer Charlie Chick's question 'How do you know what the book is about?' After a period of time, she then presented the surprising response, 'A, M, O, B, K, seven, eight, nine, ten, eleven'. This suggests that Huda may have believed that the provision of letter and number names is the *correct* response to such questions about reading.

Moreover, Huda's teacher reported that Huda 'really likes reading' and 'will often mention things like, "Mum and me likes reading" or "My mum reads the newspaper"'. It therefore seems likely that Huda was looking to her mother in particular to gain an understanding of what was meant by the terms 'being a reader' and 'doing reading'. Yet Huda did not seem to believe that the reading that she herself engaged with was the same as that of her mother. For example, when asked who she thought would be able to read a poster on the wall, Huda replied, 'I don't know [how to read it] – you have to ask mummy to read it'. What is more, even though Huda described reading as 'easy', when asked to talk about her own reading, she later placed both the *Reading words in books* card and the *Reading words on the computer* card in the 'hard' pile during the Learning Skills activity. To summarise, while in Nursery, Huda seemed to believe that reading could be defined as 'looking at' books and 'enjoying' books; within this definition she did see herself as a reader and spoke positively about reading books. Yet her comments also suggested that she was beginning to believe that there are aspects of reading that she cannot do. Bearing in mind Huda's recital of letters and numbers, this further suggests that issues relating to print literacy were about to penetrate Huda's definitions of reading.

Ibrihim, on the other hand, also seemed to regard himself as a reader and reported that it was 'easy to learn to read', but he did not appear to share Shaun's or Huda's interest or concern about the presence of print in texts. Rather, Ibrihim appeared to focus solely on the pictures in books. For example, having told Charlie Chick that 'reading is fun ... fun and good', he then volunteered to show Charlie Chick what reading is. Having chosen the book *Aladdin*, Ibrihim then used the pictures to provide Charlie Chick with a dialogue, explaining what was happening on each page. Most of the reading took this form of explanation, rather than story-telling. However, he concluded with the phrase, 'and they were so happy'.

Not only was Ibrihim using pictures to make meaning from texts, he also appeared very comfortable in doing so. For example, when Charlie Chick asked him if he liked to read words, Ibrihim dismissed the suggestion, stating that 'you need pictures and that' to read. Moreover, when later asked if you look at pictures or words when reading a book, Ibrihim confidently replied, 'You look at pictures'. While Ibrihim appeared to be clearly displaying positive views about reading and his own strategies to acquire meaning from texts, it is interesting to note that neither his teacher nor mother described him as having a particular desire to learn to read. For example, his mother reported that Ibrihim is only 'interested in books because she's [his six-year-old sister] doing it'. Furthermore, Ibrihim's teacher reported that although 'he quite enjoys books the same as the rest of them … he is not so fantastic with the phonics' and claimed that he appeared to have little interest in letters or words.

However, this is not really surprising in view of the fact that Ibrihim did not, at this stage, appear to be including print literacy within his own definition of reading. Even when faced with printed words in a variety of multidimensional contexts, such as within the Popular Culture activity, he paid little attention to the print and based his responses on factors such as contextual clues or colour. For example, when shown the printed cards in the Popular Culture activity, Ibrihim reported that each card said 'Can I come in?' Yet even though Ibrihim appeared to know that he was *guessing*, he still seemed to believe that his interpretations of what the words said was authentic reading, and appeared comfortable with this.

So far it is clear that the Nursery children who regarded themselves as readers perceived 'reading' to be many different things. Looking at books, enjoying books, reading pictures, guessing what printed words say, using context, saying letters and numbers as well as elements of print decoding all seemed to constitute a definition of 'reading' for these children. What is more, simply being 'big enough' to read appeared to be perceived as an important factor in becoming a reader. This contrasted greatly with the profiles of Caitlyn and Kelly, who both reported that reading was a 'hard' activity to learn because of a strong emphasis on the perceived need to decode print. As neither girl saw herself as able to decode print, neither girl perceived herself to be a reader. Yet in spite of this, both girls appeared to be largely positive about reading in a general sense.

Profiles: Caitlyn and Kelly

Caitlyn – aged 4 years 7 months (November birthday)
First language – English
Ethnic origin – British
Place in family – third of three

Caitlyn lives with her mother, father, six-year-old sister and nine-year-old brother. Both Caitlyn's parents work full-time. Caitlyn's mother teaches at the same school that Caitlyn attends, spending half of her week working as a class teacher and the other half supporting children for whom English is a second

(Continued)

(Continued)

language. Caitlyn is a quiet and reserved child. Caitlyn's teacher reported that Caitlyn would spend a lot of time on her own, at the beginning of the year 'in the book corner – just reading stories to herself'. Books are evidently very important to Caitlyn. Both Caitlyn's mother and teacher emphasised her 'passion' for books and ability to create story narratives from pictures.

Kelly – aged 4 years 6 months (December birthday)
First language – English
Ethnic origin – British
Place in family – first of two

Kelly lives with her mother, father and two-year-old brother. Her mother works part-time in a local department store while her father works for Royal Mail. Both of Kelly's parents and her maternal grandparents are involved in looking after Kelly and her brother. Moreover, Kelly's grandfather also helps in her Nursery one morning a week, which Kelly and her grandfather seem to enjoy. Kelly is a quiet but cheerful and sociable girl. She is described by her teacher as being 'really jolly [and] very enthusiastic about everything', and that she is a child who particularly enjoys the 'social' side of school life. Kelly's mother and teacher both reported that Kelly has a great passion for creative activities. Kelly's teacher highlighted her love of 'the creative table – colouring and drawing – things like that'. Similarly, when asked what Kelly likes to do at home, her mother reported that she enjoys 'drawing mostly … She'll do a bit of everything – but mainly drawing and cutting', while further stating that 'her favourite toy is her felt-tips'.

Perceptions of being a 'non-reader' in Nursery

Caitlyn in particular demonstrated a great passion for books, as well as an extraordinary ability to create an expressive narrative around the pictures. While her teacher described her ability to 'tell a story from a book' as 'phenomenal', her mother also reported that Caitlyn reads books constantly at home and has 'really got the hang of the narrative structure'. Caitlyn herself demonstrated this ability when asked to show Charlie Chick how to use a book. Having selected a picture book, she immediately began to expressively narrate a story based on the pictures on each page. She read:

> This big fella is going to sleep, and so is this little fella. These little fellas are playing on a hot summer day. Be careful! Don't fall in the sea. I told you! Let's go to sleep in the weeds. Fast asleep. I caught a butterfly. It's raining. It's sunny. Let's go out and play. Come on [unclear]. Oh no. I'm lost. I'd better come with her. Oh no. I'd better come that way.

Caitlyn clearly owns an exceptional ability to read pictures, yet when asked how she knew what the story was about she replied, 'I need to look at these bits (pointing to the print). And see if they sound. And if they're the right letters'. This suggests that Caitlyn was very aware of what the school system expects in terms of reading being defined as print dependent, despite the fact that both her mother and teacher spoke very positively about her picture-reading skills. What is more, both Caitlyn's mother and teacher reported that they believed Caitlyn was either unaware of print or was not especially interested in learning to decode it. Yet Caitlyn's profile suggested that not only was she very aware of how print functioned in texts, she was also quite concerned about the task of having to learn to decode print. Many of her comments referred to reading as being 'word based' which she spoke of as being 'hard' and requiring a great deal of 'practice'.

Like Caitlyn, Kelly also seemed aware of an impending expectation that she will soon have to learn to decode printed text. She too reported that learning to read is 'hard', explaining that this is because 'I can't read'. Unlike Caitlyn though, rather than this being a concern, it seemed to be something that she was looking forward to learning to do. Although she reported that she was not a reader yet, Kelly's profile suggested that she believed she would become a reader once she 'is five'. Moreover, Kelly also seemed interested in one particular aspect of letter knowledge – the letters in her name. For example, during the home visit she was observed writing her name over and over again. Her mother also reported that she 'will often point out letters that are in her own name' within the environment and will say, 'That's my name!' when finding a 'K' for example.

Although Caitlyn and Kelly both saw themselves as non-readers and viewed reading as highly dependent on learning to decode printed text, they appeared to have very different views about what 'learning to read' would mean for them as individuals. Although perceived as a difficult skill, Kelly appeared to be looking forward to learning to read print and was excited about becoming 'a reader'. Caitlyn, on the other hand, appeared much more concerned about having to learn to decode print, yet she seemed to believe that this is what she must learn to do in order to become an authentic reader.

While it was clear that the five children already discussed all appeared to have formed perceptions of themselves as either 'a reader' or 'non-reader', David's Nursery profile differed from the others in that he did not seem to be aware of an active process to *teach* or *learn* reading. Consequently, perceptions of reading at this stage appeared to be highly integrated within other aspects of daily life as now discussed.

David's story – integrated perceptions of reading

Profile: David

David – aged 4 years 7 months (November birthday)
First language – English
Ethnic origin – British
Place in family – second of two (third child expected later this year)

David lives with his mother, father and 6-year-old sister in a new development of houses close to the school. David's mother and father both work as contract cleaners. David's mother was expecting her third child at the time of the first home visit. Although one of the older children in the class, David gives the appearance of being one of the youngest. His speech is still unclear and he is physically small for his age. He is passionate about 'superheroes', which form the basis of nearly all his play and dialogue. Most of David's free play in the Nursery classroom and in the home is centred on superhero play; this includes reference to 'Batman', 'Superman', 'Power Rangers' and 'Action Man'. He is often seen dressing up in superhero clothes in the Nursery and will engage in lengthy role-play situations with his friends. Most of this role play focuses on 'fighting baddies', 'rescuing people' and 'saving the day', and involves lots of physical activity both inside and outside the classroom. When observed in his home environment, David continued to engage in role-play dialogue using his plastic superhero characters.

David's Nursery profile differed from the other children in this cohort in that he did not seem to be aware of an active process to teach or learn reading. Subsequently, perceptions of reading appeared to be highly integrated within other aspects of daily life for David. Interviews conducted during the first phase of the study suggested that David had little to say on the subject of reading. Having reported that *Learning to read words in books* was 'hard', during the Learning Skills activity, David did report that learning to read and write words on the computer was 'easy', but was unable to elaborate on any of this. When asked to show Charlie Chick what reading is, he did create a brief dialogue based on the pictures in a book about dinosaurs. When his attention was drawn to the print in the text, his gaze immediately travelled back to the pictures and he provided no comments about the role of print or pictures in texts.

Both David's teacher and mother reported that they did not believe that David had an interest in learning to read. While David's teacher reported that he will 'happily look at books on the carpet' she also stated that she does not think 'he's really aware of reading'. David's mother also reported that he is 'not interested in letters or numbers' and spoke of her reluctance to 'push' him at home as she feared he could 'end up hating' reading and writing. She therefore concluded that she would rather leave the task of learning to read to the school, where she believed David would be more willing to attempt the activity.

For David, school therefore appeared to be a place where he could largely act out superhero activity through the context of play with his friends. He did not seem to regard school in terms of teaching or learning, and did not appear to be aware of an active process to teach him to read. Yet David was evidently learning how to read iconic and printed images through the media of popular culture, play and television. This was strikingly apparent during the Popular Culture activity where David revealed an ability to match print and iconic popular culture cards together. Having initially reported that he did not recognise any of the printed cards, David clearly recognised the *CBeebies* card, in iconic form, stating that he knew this was *CBeebies* 'because I saw it in television'. Yet when told that the iconic cards matched a printed version, and asked if he could try and find the partner to the *CBeebies* card, David was unable to do so. The same process occurred with the *Bob the Builder* card, where David was able to read the iconic version but could not match it to the printed card. However, when given the iconic *Scooby Doo* card, David not only identified it as such, but immediately cried out 'That one!' while spontaneously pointing to the correct printed card. From here, David proceeded to accurately match *Barbie* and *Tweenies* before then matching the original *CBeebies* card and *Bob the Builder* card to their printed partners.

This suggests that David was indeed learning to recognise elements of printed text during his Nursery year, but was doing so within a context of popular culture and television texts, rather than ascribing to a specific schooled notion of reading. It also appeared to be the case that in terms of learning to read print, David had managed to utilise these mediums for himself without any specific adult intervention, though this was not recognised in school.

☐ Summary

This chapter has introduced the six Nursery children from The Oakfield Study and explained how they each came to develop their own unique definitions of reading as well as understandings of what is meant by the term 'being a reader'. As these cases have shown, the Nursery children drew from their own home experiences in developing their ideas and beliefs about reading. As a result, these children were seen to have formed broad definitions of the term 'reading' which included the construction of narrative using pictures and guessing at words as well as using print. Because these definitions of reading were not confined to print-decoding skills, many of these children saw themselves as readers and seemed comfortable in employing a variety of strategies to make sense of texts at home and at school. Yet in the cases of Caitlyn and Kelly, it was clear that structured definitions of reading were not only beginning to penetrate their definitions of reading, but were also prompting the children to question their own abilities in reading.

By means of comparison, the next chapter now examines the Reception children's definitions of reading. The chapter also reports on the ways in which the perceptions of all twelve children changed over the course of the year and the implications this has for early years practitioners involved in the teaching of reading in settings today.

Key questions 🔑

- Based on The Oakfield Study, what are the fundamental differences between the perceptions of the Nursery children who do and those who do not view themselves as readers at this stage?
- What could early years practitioners do to encourage each of these Nursery children to value the strategies they have developed to make sense of texts?

3

Children's perceptions of reading: defining 'reading' in Reception

Chapter Overview

The previous chapter illustrated that while many of the Nursery children in The Oakfield Study were beginning to think of reading in terms of decoding print, they still included factors such as 'reading pictures' or simply 'enjoying books' within their definitions of reading. However, in contrast to this, the Reception children all spoke about reading in terms of decoding print, even though their individual attitudes to reading and interactions with texts varied. This chapter now examines the responses of the Reception children in the study, with a view to exploring the ways in which definitions of reading can shape how children view themselves as 'readers'. The chapter concludes with a discussion, in reference to all of the children in The Oakfield Study, exploring how children's definitions of reading not only impact upon their views of themselves as 'readers', but can influence the ways in which they develop specific strategies to make sense of and engage with texts in general.

The Reception cohort

Out of the sample of six Reception children, only two described themselves as 'readers' during the early stages of the study. This chapter begins by examining the profiles of Imogen and Toby, who both reported that they were readers.

Profiles: Imogen and Toby

Imogen – aged 5 years, 8 months (October birthday)
First language – English
Ethnic origin – British
Place in family – second of two

Imogen lives with her mother (a librarian for a local college) her father and her sister Hannah who is two years her senior. Imogen is a quiet yet confident girl. She is an articulate child who has no difficulty in expressing herself and asserting her ideas. She has a close relationship with her older sister and the two girls spend much of their time playing together at home and engaging in creative activities. Imogen is a popular child in her class and has good relationships with adults and children alike. Her teacher reported that she is 'mature and very popular' and that the other children 'fight about who's going to sit next to her at lunch time'.

Toby – aged 5 years 8 months (November birthday)
First language – English
Ethnic origin – English
Place in family – first of two

Toby lives with his mother and baby brother. Toby's grandfather was reported to spend a lot of time with Toby, taking him to school each morning and taking him to the library on regular occasions. Toby is an imaginative, articulate child who regularly engages in role play both at home and in school. He has a great love of Star Wars and owns a collection of Star Wars figures. His mother reported that these figures are his favourite toys and that he spends a considerable amount of time at home playing with them. Toby's teacher describes him as a boy who is 'very keen [and] does lovely work' and is regarded as one of the more able children in the class. While his teacher also described him as having 'a good attitude towards his work', she did report that 'socially – outside – it's still a bit of a problem' as it is common for Toby to be 'in trouble' due to some dispute at playtime.

Perceptions of being 'a reader' in Reception

Both Imogen and Toby were described as being very positive about reading by their teacher and their mothers. Imogen's teacher described her as 'keen from the start' and 'not a bit apprehensive' about learning to read, while her mother reported that Imogen was 'quite laid back about it all' and stated that the process of learning to read had been 'relaxed' and 'natural'. Similarly, Toby's teacher reported that he had 'gone along and learned to read very quickly and reads beautifully', while his mother stated that he 'really enjoys' reading and reported that his progress in reading 'has been brilliant' over the course of the year.

It was apparent that both Imogen and Toby were regarded as successful readers. They were both in the top reading group during Reception and were considered to be able readers. What is more, both children appeared to *like* reading print and appeared very comfortable doing so. In fact, Toby dismissed the suggestion that pictures were especially important in reading and focused his attention almost completely on the printed text during all research activities.

In contrast, although claiming that reading is about 'understanding' words, Imogen appeared to be using a variety of strategies to make meaning from texts, including phonetic strategies, picture and contextual clues. For example, having reported that reading is 'quite easy' Imogen went on to explain that this is because 'you just look at the pictures and that gives you an idea of what the words say'. This suggests that although Imogen regarded 'reading' as being print dependent, she did not focus on *decoding* individual words. Rather, she recognised that she could derive meaning from many different sources, including the pictures, all of which could help her to understand what the words were 'saying'. This suggests that Imogen saw 'reading' as being somewhat *bigger* than the decoding of individual words, as she was more concerned with understanding the whole text. This was again emphasised when she was asked what it means if someone 'can't read'. To this she replied, 'When the teacher calls them, they can't read the book, and the teacher has to read the book to them … so they can read it back to her'. This again confirms that Imogen believed that 'reading' is about *the book* not *the words*, yet this comment also highlights a different issue: Imogen's attitude towards *school* reading.

Imogen is here suggesting that reading, in a school context, is all about the teacher calling your name and the child performing the task of reading back to the teacher. Yet she does not seem to be entirely positive about this, even though she clearly sees herself as able to read. This was further illustrated when she was asked what it means if someone is good at reading. To this Imogen replied; 'It means you just read – and get on with it, even if you don't want to read. The teacher says you need to read'. Later in the same interview Imogen also reported, 'Sometimes you just get it over with, without waiting for the teacher to tell you what the words are'. Finally, when asked during the Small World Play activity whether it is easier to 'do' reading at home or at school, she replied, 'At home because I've got my mummy to help me'. Together this suggests that even though Imogen is 'good at reading', she does not enjoy the *requirement* to read, as is enforced by school. This is discussed in more detail in later chapters.

The remaining four Reception children (Simona, Annie, Malcolm and Joseph) all reported similar definitions of reading to Toby and Imogen, in that they defined reading as the decoding of print. However, unlike Toby and Imogen, these children all appeared uncomfortable when handling print.

Profiles: Simona, Annie, Malcolm and Joseph

Simona – aged 5 years, 4 months (February birthday)
Ethnic origin – British/Chilean
First language – English/Spanish
Place in family – first of two

Simona lives with her mother, father and her 16-month-old sister. Simona's mother is from Chile and her father is English. Her mother reported that Simona learned to speak both English and Spanish simultaneously, but is 'better with her English than with her Spanish'. Simona is an articulate and creative girl, who is especially keen on drawing and writing. While her teacher reported that 'she's doing really well' in all aspects of the curriculum, she also stated that 'her writing is unbelievable' and that she can 'write for England' in that she produces 'pages and pages' of writing. Simona's teacher stressed that she enjoys drawing as well as writing and that 'she loves making books and is quite passionate about it'. At home, Simona appears to enjoy a variety of activities, with her mother reporting that Simona enjoys 'doing painting [and] colouring' when she is at home, as well as 'playing 'schools'.

Annie – 5 years 0 months (June birthday)
First language – English
Ethnic origin – English
Place in family – first and only

Annie lives with her mother. She is a lively and cheerful girl, with a passion for Barbie dolls. She spends a lot of time at home creating scenarios with the dolls and engaging in role-play situations. Annie's mother reported that Annie will play with her dolls 'for hours' while her teacher reported that 'she particularly enjoys role play'. It appears that while Annie now integrates very well into the school environment and has many friends, her teacher reported that she was a 'very shy child' when she began Reception and did not want to participate in school life. Annie's mother spoke very positively about school, both in terms of the Reception year and the potential for years to come.

Claiming that she herself was 'so unhappy' at school, she reported that she wants Annie 'to enjoy her school … enjoy her school mates' as well as experience academic success. Annie's mother also reported that she herself left school when she was in Year 9 and therefore did not sit any exams because she 'didn't really care', yet she stated that she wants Annie to be successful at school.

Malcolm – aged 4 years 11 months (August birthday)
First language – English
Ethnic origin – English/American
Place in family – first of two

Malcolm lives with his mother, father and three-year-old sister. The family moved to England from Los Angeles two years ago, partly because Malcolm's parents were unhappy with the school system in Los Angeles at that time. Malcolm is a very quiet, slightly timid child, who on occasions has quite a profound stammer. Malcolm is the youngest child in his class. Both Malcolm's mother and teacher gave comments suggesting that they felt Malcolm was disadvantaged by being so young in his year. Malcolm enjoys drawing and colouring. He is also passionate about soft toys which he often uses to structure role-play scenarios with his sister.

Joseph – aged 5 years 4 months
First language – English
Ethnic origin – English (father of Afro/Caribbean origin)
Place in family – first and only

Joseph lives with his mother. However, his maternal grandparents live close by and have regular contact with Joseph and his mother. Joseph also has regular contact with his father although this relationship was not discussed in any great detail. Joseph is a very cheerful, energetic and articulate child, described by his teacher as a 'nice child' with 'a really kind heart'. He is passionate about racing cars, which is an interest encouraged by his maternal grandfather who races cars regularly. He is a very active child who is reported to need a lot of physical play within his daily routine. Joseph attends after-school club three days a week while his mother is at work. He seems to enjoy the experience and talks about the club in positive terms. Joseph is an avid user of digital technology. Though he does not have a computer at home, he reported that he uses the computer regularly at school and at after-school club.

Perceptions of being 'a non-reader' in Reception

While Simona, Annie, Malcolm and Joseph all shared Imogen's and Toby's belief that 'reading' was about decoding print, their comments suggested that they believed learning to read print was difficult and

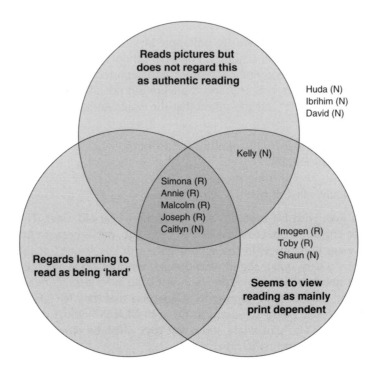

Figure 3.1 Perceptions of reading as an ability to read pictures and print (Phase 1)

they all seemed quite uncomfortable with the process. For example, all four children categorised *Learning to read words in books* as 'hard', during the Learning Skills activity. Moreover, with the exception of Joseph, all of these children also reported that *Learning to read words on the computer* should be placed in the 'hard' pile. While all of these children also demonstrated an ability to access meaning from texts by using pictures, they all reported that they did not believe this to be 'real' authentic reading (see Figure 3.1).

For example, having volunteered to tell Charlie Chick what reading is by giving him a description of the process, Simona told him, 'Well you read and you – you look at the picture and you act like a big boy or a big girl, properly with books'. Yet when asked if she could show Charlie Chick what reading is, she became very hesitant, stating, 'Read it. I can't actually read hard … really books. But I can read short books that … are at school – but these are really hard'. When asked if she could read a 'Kipper book' (a book from the Oxford Reading Tree) she nodded, but then pointed to the picture books and reiterated, 'But I can't read these books'.

Despite this reported hesitancy, Simona demonstrated that she was highly competent in using pictures to create an expressive narrative when she later agreed to show Charlie Chick how to read a picture book. Having selected a lift-the-flap book, which featured a variety of colourful egg-shaped flaps to lift, the following extract from the interview transcript provides an example of the narrative she created.

> And the duck said, 'What a beautiful egg'. The baby chick was so upset – he couldn't find food. But the mummy said, 'You can be my baby, so let's find something to eat'. And there was an Easter egg. Next they went together … with a king. There was a purple egg … and a pink one. (Simona, Phase 1)

Although competent in using pictures to create a narrative, Simona clearly did not accept that this was 'proper' reading. Having consistently reported that a reader is someone who has 'learned' and has become 'clever enough', there was much in Simona's profile to suggest that she perceives reading to be largely about *reading words*. To further illustrate, when presented with the printed versions of the Popular Culture cards she again appeared almost worried about what was expected of her. She asked, 'If I don't know it … can I … can I just … say the word that I know?' Once reassured that she did not have to say anything unless she wanted to, Simona happily pointed out the word 'the' within the *Bob the Builder* and the *Thomas the Tank Engine* cards. She then used her knowledge of phonetics to provide clues as to what the other cards might say, for example suggesting that *Scooby Doo* might read as 'some day'.

Like Simona, Annie also appeared to separate picture reading from reading printed text in terms of definition. Having reported that she had once 'tried to read a book' but 'can't read books', Annie asked if she could 'show him [Charlie Chick] the pictures' rather than show him how to read. She then explained to Charlie Chick that 'we need pictures to look at' in books, but claimed that the print is for 'reading'. This suggests that Annie does not see the pictures as contributing towards reading. She regards pictures as necessary in order to have something pleasant to 'look' at, but did not appear to regard them as tools to help access the meaning of texts. This contrasts sharply with Imogen who, although a competent reader of printed text, appeared to view pictures as very much part of the *whole* text, and reported that she uses pictures and print together to access meaning from books.

Another issue raised by these particular Reception children related to the fact that they all regarded reading as an ability to 'read books', rather

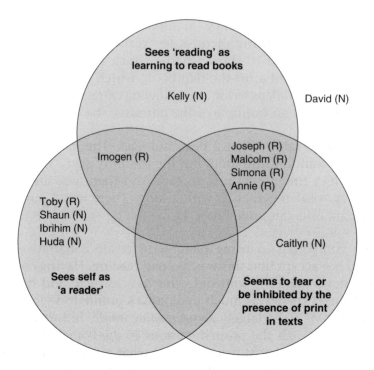

Figure 3.2 Perceptions of reading as an ability to read books (Phase 1)

than read any other material. As demonstrated in Figure 3.2, with one exception from within each cohort, the Nursery children did not report that reading was about being able to 'read books', while the Reception children reported that this was indeed the case. However, the four children who claimed that they were not readers also reported that they were unable to read books and provided comments that suggested that they either feared or were inhibited by the presence of print in texts.

Given that Simona, Annie, Joseph and Malcolm all reported that they were unable to read books (and that 'reading' is an ability to 'read books'), questions arise with regard to the actual books themselves. In particular, it seems appropriate to ask, 'Which books do children see themselves as able or unable to read and how does this affect their perceptions of themselves as readers?' As already highlighted, Simona stated that she could not 'read hard … books', but could only 'read short books' which were from her reading scheme. This suggests that Simona did not see herself as a reader at this stage, because she was unable to read books that extended *beyond* her reading scheme. In other words, Simona appeared to believe that a reader was someone who could read books that existed outside of the reading scheme.

Similarly, having already reported that learning to read is 'hard' because 'I can't read books yet', when asked to show Charlie Chick what reading is, Malcolm chose to demonstrate the activity by using a reading scheme book, despite there being a variety of books on the table from which he could choose. What is more, he was adamant that he could not read the picture books. This again suggests that like Simona, Malcolm felt that the only book he could attempt to read was a reading scheme book, although he was evidently concerned about being unable to read this too. Moreover, Malcolm also reported that reading is 'when the teacher calls your name and you have to read to your teacher and at home your mummy and daddy reads to you'. This suggests that Malcolm regards reading scheme books as instrumental in teaching children to *perform* the task of reading to the teacher. The role of reading scheme texts in shaping children's perceptions of themselves as readers is discussed in greater detail in the next chapter.

Like Simona, Joseph too reported that he 'can't read hard ... [but] can only read the school books that are easy – and a bit hard'. Further, when asked what reading is, Joseph reported that, 'It means you have to learn lots of books'. What is more, Joseph went on to explain that reading is also when 'you have to do group reading'. This suggests that in concurrence with data gathered from the other Reception children who did not see themselves as readers, Joseph too believed that 'reading' is about learning to read specific books within the reading scheme. Like Malcolm, Joseph is suggesting that learning to read is about performing a task, in this case within the context of 'group reading', which he asserts 'helps you learn to read so you know some of the books'.

Reading words, reading pictures, reading whole texts

Having now introduced the twelve children in the study, it is clear that the Nursery children generally entered the schooling system with broad and holistic definitions of reading in comparison with the Reception children, who all reported far narrower constructions. The Reception children all defined 'reading' as being almost exclusively the acquisition of print-literacy skills. Reading was largely seen to be the decoding of print in books, often manifest in presenting a 'correct' performance to the teacher in school. As most of the Reception children saw themselves as unable to decode print in this way, they did not believe themselves to be readers.

Moreover, given this emphasis on print-decoding, most of the children in the Reception cohort reported a reluctance to include other meaning-making strategies, such as picture-reading skills, within their definitions. Yet the role of picture reading has been emphasised by researchers and educationalists as a vital contribution to children's early development in reading. For example, having analysed children's responses to picture books over the course of a two-year in-depth study, Arizpe and Styles (2003: 224) demonstrated that pictures not only provide pleasure and motivation for children of all ages, but that the reading of pictures is 'an intellectual activity'. Similarly, Walsh (2003: 123) argued that 'images can evoke different levels of response' and concluded that the reading of pictures is a different process from the reading of words. This is not to say that researchers are arguing that picture and print reading should be treated as separate elements in a text; on the contrary they are suggesting that the relationship between the two can be both complex and stimulating. Lewis (2001) points out that pictures in picture books act upon the words in a whole variety of ways, before going on to specify that pictures might provide the reader with an expansion or an enlargement of the words, an alternative to the words or even a contradiction.

Nikolajeva and Scott also emphasise the broad spectrum of word/image interaction occurring in picture books. With specific reference to integrated picture books, where the author provides the pictures as well as the printed text instead of the book being illustrated by a second party, the authors highlight the complex dynamics between word and image which can 'collaborate to communicate meanings beyond the scope of either one alone' (2000: 226). Like Lewis, Nikolajeva and Scott argue that the relationship between words and pictures can at times be contradictory, challenging the reader to mediate between the two in order to establish a valid understanding. Moreover, in reference to the work of Stephen Behrendt (1996), Garrett-Petts (2000) goes on to describe the combination of words and images as a 'third text' or an 'interdisciplinary "metatext"'. He argues that pictures in texts often do far more than simply illustrate a point, but function 'as a form of embedded interpretation, elucidating or otherwise complicating our responses'. Work such as this suggests that readers must work hard to make connections between words and pictures, thus emphasising the importance of developing both picture- and print-reading skills, as well as skills of mediation between the two. Yet despite the fact that children appear to develop abilities to use elements of 'visual grammar' (Kress and van Leeuwen, 1996: 4) with relative ease, many fear that this intellectual tool, often used intrinsically by young children to find meaning in texts, is greatly undervalued in schools.

This seems to stem, at least in part, from the fact that teachers often regard the use of pictures in children's reading and writing as something of a prop to be used until the 'real' skills of print literacy are developed. As Millard and Marsh argue, 'teachers largely regard the movement from pictures to words as one of intellectual progression' (2001: 55). This means that the visual elements of text reading can be seen to lose status in schools. Moreover, as Garrett-Petts (2000) points out, emphasis in schools on print literacy may actually encourage a degree of 'visual illiteracy'. He argues that pedagogies of reading encourage the illustrations to be viewed as a 'blank' in their subordination to the print in the text. Yet he reasons that if readers are not proficient in reading the visual, then they will miss out on 'much of the best writing'.

Certainly results from The Oakfield Study indicate that there is good reason for these concerns to be acknowledged. Findings from this study revealed that young children at the beginning of their school careers were already coming to believe that their picture-reading skills were not authentic and did not contribute towards a definition of real 'reading'. As the children moved up a class during the year of data collection, it became clear that the Nursery cohort in particular experienced changes in their constructions of what was meant by the terms 'reading' and being 'a reader', with their definitions of the terms narrowing. Shaun, for example, was evidently using a variety of strategies to make meaning from texts during his Nursery year. Though he was able to decode some aspects of printed text, and clearly had an interest in letters and words, he did not seem to believe that print should be considered more 'important' than pictorial images in books. What is more, he appeared to be including print-reading *and* picture-reading skills within his definition of 'reading'. Yet in the second phase of the study, once Shaun was established in Reception, he reported that looking at pictures is 'kind of reading' but could no longer be considered as actual reading. In fact Shaun no longer appeared to be including picture reading within his definition of reading, stating that this was not 'real' reading because 'mostly it's just looking at the pictures'. Furthermore, when told during the final phase of the study that Charlie Chick could read the iconic Popular Culture cards, but not the printed versions, and asked if he was therefore 'a reader', Shaun replied that 'He can't read yet because he can't read those [pointing to the printed versions of the cards]'.

As highlighted in the first section of this chapter, although clearly concerned that her reading was not authentic, Caitlyn demonstrated an exceptional ability to construct a detailed narrative based upon the pictures in her books in the first phase of the study. Yet in contrast with this, when asked to show Charlie Chick what reading was during the second phase of the study she provided a highly instructional account of what 'reading' is. Having reported that a particular feature of books is that 'lots of them have "the" in them', she went on to describe how one must look for specific letters within the printed text. Speaking of the letter 'K' she reported:

> And now here it is again – the same as in that book ... and a 'd' is there and there – and you can see it here ... and you can find it in the middle of something and it is a bit hard to write it. 'K' is on lots of pages on books ... because it's in the middle and it begins lots of things.

It is startling how Caitlyn's demonstration of reading has gone from the highly expressive and complex narrative structure reported earlier to this benign account of 'letter-spotting' now that she is in Reception. What is more, even though Caitlyn maintained a great deal of interest in the reading of pictures, the latter stages of data collection suggest that she became reluctant to even acknowledge that picture reading has much of a role in authentic reading. Not only did she largely ignore the pictures when asked to show Charlie Chick what reading is, but when asked if pictures help children to read, she replied, 'Sometimes – but not all the time'. She then clarified that 'when you start to learn sounds [then] you get to learn to read'.

Once in Reception, Caitlyn did still seem to enjoy reading pictures in books, but did not appear to regard this as 'reading'. For example, when observed during an independent reading activity, Caitlyn became very absorbed in the book she had selected, running her finger over the pictures and creating narratives. She engaged in an animated dialogue, created from the pictures, giving no attention at all to the printed text. Yet when asked to focus on print, as was often observed during whole-class and group activities, she was evidently uncertain about the printed text. For example, during a guided reading activity, Caitlyn seemed very insecure with the text, often waiting for another child to respond before joining in with the group to answer the teacher's questions. She was largely very quiet and reserved until at one point, towards the end of the session, she spotted something of interest to her in one of the pictures. Caitlyn's reaction to this is captured in the field notes taken during the observation:

The teacher is reading the sentence 'The cat jumped over the oranges' when Caitlyn suddenly exclaims 'Look!' She is pointing to some detail in the pictures. Over the next few minutes Caitlyn remains quite excited and speaks with animation about some specific detail she has noticed in the picture. When the teacher then asks the group a question about the picture Caitlyn volunteers an answer without hesitation.

This suggests that Caitlyn still wants to focus on the pictures in books and is able to derive much meaning from them. Yet she tries very hard to decode print, especially within a school context, as she believes this is what is expected of her. What is more, in the final phase of data collection Caitlyn's mother reported that when it comes to reading, Caitlyn continues to prefer 'to make it [the narrative] up' at home, using the pictures, because she does not 'see herself as great' at decoding print. This suggests that as Caitlyn has moved through the early stages of formal schooling, a dichotomy has continued to widen between her constructions of 'schooled' and 'home' discourses on reading. This is a crucial issue and will be discussed in detail in Chapter 6.

Unlike Caitlyn, Kelly appeared to be much more confident about learning to read print when in Nursery. However, this confidence seemed to diminish somewhat during her Reception year. For example, when asked to show Charlie Chick what reading is during the second phase of the study, she chose not to show him what reading is but elected to describe it instead, stating that it is 'when you point at words and look at them and tell what they are'. However, she went on to report that she was unable to do this. When asked if it was alright to look at the pictures, she replied that 'we can look at pictures if we want' but stated that it is the 'writing' that tells us what is happening in a book. It therefore appears that Kelly had become less confident in her abilities as a reader once in Reception, as she did not see herself as able to decode 'words' as was now expected.

This same issue was raised in the final phase of data collection when Kelly's mother reported that Kelly does 'enjoy' reading her schoolbook to her every day, but that she enjoys 'telling the story even more' from her own books in the home. Kelly's mother went on to report that they have 'plenty' of their own 'longer books' in the house which Kelly very much enjoys reading. She further explained that when Kelly is reading these books she is 'not reading word for word, but she'll look at the pictures' and will be 'putting quite a lot of expression in'. Kelly's mother then drew a contrast between this and Kelly's reading of her school books, which she reported as being 'quite monotonous', unlike the reading of her home books because 'when she's reading from her head she uses quite a lot of expression'.

This suggests that definitions of reading formed before entry into Reception provided valuable territory for these young children to develop understandings about texts and confidences in themselves as readers. Yet these constructions were disrupted by the narrow discourse on reading operating within the school system. As the Nursery children moved into Reception, like the Reception cohort, they all came to believe that 'reading' was all about decoding print in books. While for some children, like Shaun, a retained interest in phonics meant that the transition into Reception was less problematic; for children like Caitlyn and Kelly, the move into Reception proved far more contentious. As their own constructions of reading failed to fit with those of the school, they appeared to lose confidence in themselves as readers. What is more, both girls were clearly developing a variety of strategies within their home contexts in order to make meaning from whole texts and gain pleasure from these interactions, yet the narrow focus on decoding words in Reception threatened to disrupt such progression.

Surely it should be a priority for all early years educators to promote wide and meaningful interactions with texts? This issue was raised by Lysaker (2006) who used wordless picture books with 18 children aged 5 and 6 to understand how children enter the 'text world' and 'make sense of it through a personal, relational experience' (2006: 33). By understanding the different ways in which the children positioned themselves within the texts, Lysaker asserted that through their 'dialogic capacities' children were able to engage with the texts and make sense of them. Subsequently she argued that the early years setting should provide many meaningful opportunities for children 'to take on the roles of make believe characters in symbolic play' as this in itself offers opportunity 'to develop capacities necessary for reading' (2006: 51). In other words, Lysaker is arguing that not only does symbolic play influence later literacy development, but that reading is a holistic activity in the early years, centred on children's own dialogic capacities to engage with all aspects of textual stimuli. This was evident throughout The Oakfield Study. However, the importance of such interaction was especially manifest in David's profile. This next section demonstrates how for this one child in particular definitions of 'reading' were only meaningful when embedded within a broad and interactive context. Yet the demands of a school-based curriculum served to disrupt such valuable constructions and prevent this child from engaging with the activity in a meaningful way.

David's story: schooled reading – devoid of meaning

As discussed in the first half of this chapter, David was clearly learning to recognise elements of printed text during his Nursery year, but was doing so within a context of popular culture and television texts, rather than ascribing to a specific 'schooled' notion of reading. It was especially striking to note that even though he appeared to be making little sense of print within most paper-based contexts, David was indeed able to match most of the iconic cards to their printed partners during the Popular Culture activity. Yet when this activity was repeated during the second phase of the study, David was no longer able to match any of the pairs.

This suggests that entry into Reception appeared to have a negative effect upon David's interactions with print. Although it is not possible to claim exactly why this was the case, there is much in David's profile to suggest that constructions of reading operating in the Reception classroom not only bore little meaning for him, but actually impeded his own interactions with print. David's Nursery profile demonstrated that he was developing understandings of print through the media of popular culture, television texts and play, yet schooled print reading appeared to have little meaning for David at this stage, as was observed during a particular guided reading activity.

This session was centred on the Oxford Reading Tree book *Hide and Seek*. The teaching assistant who was leading the session began by engaging the children in a general discussion about playing the game 'Hide and Seek'. David joined in the discussion with enthusiasm and was keen to share his experiences of playing 'Hide and Seek' at home. As the activity progressed, and the children's attention was drawn to the book, David remained highly engaged with the pictures. He pointed to a picture that showed Dad hiding in a tree, and then talked about the different places where people could have hidden themselves within the context of the story. As the teaching assistant turned the pages of her book, David became very excited as he realised that Dad was falling further and further out of the tree with each successive picture in the book, and talked about this with confidence and excitement to the rest of the group. However, when each of the children were then given their own copy of the book and asked to point to the words while the teaching assistant read aloud, David appeared to be at a loss, as documented in these observation notes.

> David looks at his book with confusion and seems unsure of where he is expected to point. His finger drifts randomly over the print and

he does not know when to turn the page. He then seems especially confused when faced with two pages, each with a line of print on each page. He does not appear to know which page should be read first. The teaching assistant directs him towards the print on each page ... but he appears to tire of the activity very quickly and his gaze keeps lifting from the book to the teaching assistant. He closes his book before the teaching assistant has finished reading, then realising his mistake he opens the book again quickly but does not know where to point. His expression is puzzled and he appears unsure about what to do next.

David's interactions with books were clearly extending far and beyond the minutiae of the print at this stage. In other words, 'reading' was very much about accessing the *whole text* rather than struggling to decode print, which appeared to have little meaning for him within this context. Not surprisingly, data collected in the final stage of the study suggested that this continued to be the case through to the conclusion of David's Reception year. For example, when asked about David's interest in reading, David's Reception teacher gave the following statement. She reported:

Often when he's reading a book with me, what he wants to do is talk about the things that the book reminds him of. Or talk about Spiderman in relation to that book – that kind of thing.

This again highlights that David finds meaning in stories by making broader applications to his own life or relating certain features within the texts to elements of popular culture and superhero play. Moreover, there is evidence to suggest that just as David was seen to be developing understandings about print within such contexts during his Nursery year, this continued into Reception when the print appeared within a meaningful context. For example, David was told that the researcher would read *George and the Dragon* to him at the end of the final stage interview, given that he had voiced a particular interest in the book. As the book was opened, David's gaze fell from the picture to the print where he immediately began reading the first few words, 'Far a...way'. As the book was read to David, his gaze roamed from the pictures to the print and very often remained focused on the print for a considerable length of time, even though there was no expectation for him to read the print himself. He then proceeded to repeat every sentence as it was read to him, yet while doing this, he maintained a high level of engagement with the actual plot in the story, asking extended questions such as, 'Why do all dragons do that?'

This engagement with print, pictures and overall story stands in sharp contrast to David's confusion and bewilderment when asked to point to the print in the reading scheme book during the observed guided reading activity. Similarly, having reported that David 'never sits down and looks at his schoolbook' when at home and will only do so 'sort of by force', David's mother did state that 'he's got his Spiderman books upstairs and he'll look at those'. This again suggests that schooled reading, with its emphasis on the decoding of print and attainment in mastering the reading of reading scheme books, not only has little meaning for David at present, but could also be seen to have impeded his own broader interactions with print. Yet when given the space and opportunity to interact with texts in a meaningful way, David seemed to be making sense of print as well as enjoying the interaction with the text.

☐ Summary

This chapter has explored young children's perceptions and definitions of reading at the time of entry into the formal education system. On the basis of findings from The Oakfield Study, it was revealed that Nursery children owned broader constructions of reading than Reception children, and as a result were more likely to accept strategies such as picture reading into their definitions of reading. However, once all these children entered Reception, these valuable constructions were overridden by the domination of the school discourse on reading. Despite the fact that many of the children were clearly learning much about ways in which to find meaning from texts, as well as developing confidence and motivations for reading through the context of their own 'home' discourse, the children quickly came to believe that 'real' reading was situated in the decoding of print in books. As a consequence, many of the children in this study came to believe that they were 'non-readers' or 'poor readers' from their earliest years in school, because they believed they were unable to fulfil the demands of the school discourse in reading.

Given that such definitions of reading emphasised the need to decode print *in books*, the next chapter now examines the specific role of books within perceived definitions of reading and explores how reading scheme texts in particular can shape children's perceptions of themselves as readers. The final chapters of this book look closely at the implications of these issues towards the teaching and learning of reading in schools today. However, this chapter raises some particular questions for teachers to consider when working in early years settings.

Key questions 🔑

- How can we encourage young children entering the school system to value the strategies they bring into school to make sense of text?
- How can we encourage children to form identities and relationships with texts on the basis of their own experiences and interests?
- How can we promote print-reading skills within meaningful contexts such as play and popular culture?
- How can we ensure that definitions of reading do not become dominated by a focus on decoding skills during the Foundation Stage and that young children are given opportunities to build upon their own strategies to make sense of texts during their early years in school?

Perceived uses and affordances of book texts

Chapter Overview

It stands to reason that in order to be a reader, one must be a reader of text. It is therefore easy to agree with Goodwin's (2008: 35) assertion that 'texts matter' in the process of learning to be a reader. In reference to Margaret Meek's iconic book *How Texts Teach What Readers Learn* (1988), Goodwin argues that Meek 'showed beyond doubt that … texts themselves play an important role in teaching children (and older people too) to be readers, rather than merely people who can read'. Given that Meek published this book over twenty years ago, it is not surprising that her definition of 'text' appears to pertain largely to those of paper-based origins, yet the relevance of the message remains unchanged. As raised in the Introduction, the term 'text' no longer relates to just paper-based media such as books and magazines, but includes the 'new textual landscapes' (Carrington, 2005: 13) of digital and screen-based contexts. Yet as seen in the previous chapter, the young children in The Oakfield Study defined reading as the ability to not only decode print, but decode print in *books*. This suggests that despite changes in 'textual landscape', books continue to play an important role in the development of children's self-perceptions in reading. This chapter (and the next) examines how texts themselves play a role in shaping young children's perceptions of reading. This chapter specifically explores the ways in which book texts are viewed and perceived in terms of what they offer the reader. In other words, books are examined in terms of 'affordance'. This chapter begins by examining how book texts can influence children's definitions of reading and self-perceptions of being 'a reader'. As reading scheme texts are highlighted as a major influence in the development of self-perception in reading, this is discussed in detail in the final sections of this chapter.

Term	Definition
Reading scheme	Reading schemes are graded sets of books and teaching materials that gradually expose children to more complex vocabulary
Oxford Reading Tree	The Oxford Reading Tree is one specific reading scheme that has achieved particular popularity
Real books	The term 'real books' has been used by certain educationalists to describe books, particularly fictional texts, that are not part of a reading scheme
Free reader	A child who has completed all the stages in the reading scheme and can choose freely from books in the classroom
Chapter books	Books, usually structured into chapters, that children are encouraged to read once they have completed the stages of the reading scheme
Floppy and Kipper	Characters in the Oxford Reading Tree
Independent reading	Time in the classroom when children are encouraged to read books by themselves
Guided reading	Structured reading activity conducted in small groups where children are all working from multiple copies of the same text

Figure 4.1   Definition of terms

Given that aspects of particular terminology (such as reading schemes) may not be familiar to everyone, Figure 4.1 provides definitions of some specific terms used in this chapter.

The affordance and uses of books

As observed in the previous chapter, by the time they were in Reception, all of the children in The Oakfield Study seemed to equate definitions of reading with the need to decode print. What is more, many of the children further reported that they believed that reading scheme books were highly instrumental in *teaching* reading, therefore providing the territory to learn to decode print in books. Given that reading schemes are deliberately designed to introduce children to increasingly more complex vocabulary, this perception is perhaps of no great surprise in itself. However, results from this study strongly suggested that these constructions of reading did have serious implications for the children's overall interactions with books as well as their general attitudes towards reading.

This is illustrated by returning to Malcolm's profile. Like many of the other children in The Oakfield Study, Malcolm consistently selected a reading scheme book when asked to show Charlie Chick what reading is, even though there was always a variety of books available from which to choose during the activities. In the second phase of the study he appeared very hesitant in his attempt to read the scheme book to Charlie Chick and was clearly concerned that he was unable to 'sound out' the words with accuracy, having reported that reading scheme books are 'actually reading books – books you read'. Despite the fact that Malcolm continued to report that 'reading', was about 'sounding out' words in his reading scheme text, by the third phase of the study Malcolm was himself demonstrating a substantial interest in non-fiction material, which did not appear to sit comfortably with these definitions of reading.

Over the years there has been much written on the subject of boys' interactions with non-fiction texts. Although reporting that fiction is popular with boys and girls, Millard (1997) argues that boys tend to have a particular interest in non-fiction material, while Hall and Coles (1997; 1999) have suggested that boys' home reading tends to be 'information-rich', and that schools should include more non-fiction material in the curriculum in order to engage the interest of boys. However, further research has challenged these assumptions, arguing that some boys' preference for non-fiction material may be more directly related to issues of proficiency grading than book choice. In her study of approximately 120 children in the 7–9 age group, Moss (2000: 101) found that boys and girls reacted differently to judgements made about their reading and that 'this in turn has far more impact on their respective progress in reading than the inclusion of their preferred reading materials'. Having reported that publishers and teachers tend to grade fictional texts, whether they are part of a scheme or not, Moss discovered that weaker boy readers tended to choose non-fiction texts in order to eschew proficiency grading, as the focus of the texts was on content rather than ability in reading.

Malcolm's own interest in non-fiction material became increasingly apparent over the course of the study. For example, during the Book-bag branch-activity Malcolm reported that, from the books on display, Charlie Chick would prefer to read the information books because 'he can learn much more' from these books in comparison with the others (reading scheme books and fictional texts). What is more, Malcolm's mother reported that Malcolm's 'big thing at the moment is the dog collection' which is 'a magazine that you buy once a fortnight'. This concurred with Malcolm's clear interest in animals in general, given that his mother also spoke of his attraction to 'animals and animal programmes' on the television. Malcolm's perceptions of the affordance of texts was further evidenced when he went on to report that his teacher would prefer that he read reading scheme books and non-fiction books, stating that non-fiction texts 'tell you about all the things you need to know' while reading scheme books 'would tell you how to read'. To some extent this supports Moss' assertion, as Malcolm clearly believes that reading scheme books teach reading while non-fiction texts are free from issues of proficiency in reading and simply provide the territory in which to learn about the 'real' things in the world.

Yet Malcolm appeared to value non-fiction texts, not just because they were free from proficiency grading but because they offered this knowledge of the world. This was further confirmed by the fact that Malcolm appeared quite frustrated with fictional material which he regarded as being almost deceptive. For example, when first presented with the selection of books including *George and the Dragon* (a picture book), he stated that he was less interested in this book because 'there's really no such things as dragons [but] there is such a thing as lights' (the subject of the non-fiction book). What is more, when asked if fictional texts help children learn how to read he hesitantly replied that they sometimes do, but then claimed that the problem is that 'they start telling lies, like there's such things as dragons'.

This highlights several important issues. In terms of affordance, reading scheme books were seen to *teach* reading, whereas other books were not. As a result, Malcolm not only appeared more comfortable with non-scheme books (non-fiction texts in particular) but seemed to believe that he did not have to decode the print in these texts. Similar ideas were echoed in Simona's comments who, like many of the other children, also spoke of reading scheme books as tools for teaching reading. Like Malcolm, she too selected an Oxford Reading Tree book when asked to show Charlie Chick what reading was, but rather than read it herself she used it to actually *teach* the puppet how to read.

By the third phase of the study, Simona and Malcolm were reported as being very different in terms of confidence and ability in reading. For example, the children's teacher reported that Malcolm finds reading 'very hard' and was therefore in the lowest reading group, whereas Simona was described as being 'highly competent' and was in one of the top reading groups. Despite these differences though, both children reported similar beliefs about the affordances of reading scheme texts in comparison with other books, even though Simona clearly enjoyed fictional texts far more than Malcolm.

Having stated that reading scheme books exist so as to 'teach' reading, Simona reported that she thought these were the books that Charlie Chick's teacher and parents would prefer him to read, even though she reported that Charlie Chick would himself prefer to read the 'story book'. Furthermore, when asked if Charlie Chick would be expected to read every word in his reading scheme book she replied 'Yes, he has to read every word'. When the question was repeated in relation to story books, however, Simona replied that it does 'not matter so much with those, because they're just story books'. Similarly, she stated that it was acceptable to make up the odd word in a story book, but 'not in these [reading scheme] books'. This suggests that Simona not only regards reading scheme texts in highly instructional terms, but believes that these books must be read in a different way to other books. Similarly, when Shaun was asked whether Charlie Chick looks at the words, pictures, or both when reading the picture books, during the second phase of the study Shaun reported that he looks at 'the words and the pictures'. This was also deemed to be the case for the non-fiction texts. However, when asked which bits of the text Charlie Chick would look at when reading his reading scheme book to his teacher, Shaun reported that he would look at 'the words'. This suggests that not only does Shaun regard reading scheme books as synonymous with schooled reading, he also now regards schooled reading as being heavily *word* focused. This is quite different to Shaun's Nursery profile, where he reported that you 'needed both' print and pictures in texts in order to make meaning.

This final point raises some particularly important and worrying issues. Firstly, if children believe that 'learning to read' is really about learning to decode print in reading scheme texts, this raises serious concerns about the ways in which young children develop strategies to make sense of texts. For example, research on the use of pictures in children's literature indicates that the reading of pictures in books is 'an intellectual activity' (Arizpe and Styles, 2003) and that pictures provide young readers with challenges and opportunities for reflection as well as pleasure (Lysaker, 2006). Yet if children believe that reading scheme books teach reading and that this reading must focus primarily on the decoding of print, and that picture reading is unimportant, then it seems highly possible that some children may be missing out on developing the interactive skills needed to make sense of texts in general. Lewis points out that picture reading is a crucial element of the reading process, arguing that it is inaccurate to assume that 'what pictures do to words is the same as what words do to pictures' (2001: 95) and that pictures act upon words in a whole variety of ways including an expansion or enlargement of the words, or even alternatives and contradiction

Secondly, if children regard reading scheme books as highly instrumental in teaching reading, and believe that these books must be rigorously decoded in a way that differs from the reading of other texts, one must consider how these perceptions influence children's relationships with books outside of the reading scheme. Moreover, how do these perceptions of the affordances of texts influence children's developing perceptions of themselves as readers? In order to answer these questions, we must examine how perceptions of reading scheme texts are linked to perceived issues of reading instruction and proficiency grading.

Reading scheme texts: proficiency grading and becoming 'a reader'

While it must be acknowledged that Oakfield Primary School did make substantial use of one particular reading scheme, that being the Oxford Reading Tree, there is evidence to suggest that 'reading schemes are widely used' (Solity and Vousden, 2009: 472) in UK schools. Having identified that 'the PNS (Primary National Strategy) has reinforced the role of phonics in teaching reading, and implicitly the use of reading schemes, through Letters and Sounds (DfES, 2007)'(2009: 472), Solity and Vousden go on to argue that while there is a 'considerable research base demonstrating the benefits of teaching children phonological and phonic skills', the assumption that this 'is best done through the type of restricted, controlled vocabulary that characterise reading schemes' (2009: 474) remains unfounded. In fact in their detailed analysis of reading scheme texts and 'real books', these authors 'revealed that real books offered children the same opportunities to develop sight vocabulary and phonic skills as the reading scheme texts' (Levy, 2009b: 365).

The debate surrounding whether children are better served by learning to read through the use of reading schemes or 'real books' has existed for some time. Generally perceived to be a reaction to the more structured approaches to the teaching of reading, 'the real book approach' was pioneered by Waterland in 1985, and involved using 'real books' in the teaching of reading rather than reading scheme material. However, tensions about the extent to which phonics instruction should be used to drive the reading curriculum can be identified a decade earlier in the

Bullock Report (DES, 1975). Of course, as discussed in Chapter 1, it would be naive to suggest that teachers have used either approach in isolation. However, as Solity and Vousden point out, 'there is a clear move towards teaching reading through phonics and structured reading schemes rather than real books' (2009: 472). This appears to be related to the fact that 'low standards' in literacy have been attributed to the poor quality of children's phonic skills (Ofsted, 1996; DfEE, 2001; DfES, 2003).

Yet Solity and Vousden go on to argue that as real books have 'the same structure and representation of core skills as reading schemes', they provide better opportunities for children to 'map newly acquired phonic and sight vocabulary skills to texts' (2009: 502) as well as offering children greater choice. This research has further suggested that a number of disadvantages may be associated with the use of reading scheme books. Indeed, as Luke, Carrington and Kapitzke assert, not only do reading schemes place 'limits on vocabulary, lexical density and syntactic complexity' (2003: 252), they can also be highly influential in shaping what 'counts' as literacy. Solity and Vousden raise similar concerns including the fact that the systemic structure of the schemes can encourage children and parents to 'see the primary goal of reading as being to get through the reading scheme and become a "free reader", rather than being to derive meaning and enjoyment from what is read' (2009: 502).

Findings from The Oakfield Study strongly indicated that this was exactly the case. For example, to return to Simona's profile, when shown a particular book from the Oxford Reading Tree during the second phase of the study, Simona declared, 'I'm past that stage', before going on to clarify that she had completed nearly all of the stages in the reading scheme and was 'nearly on books with black and white pages'. At the beginning of the third phase of data collection, Simona's teacher confirmed that Simona 'wants to learn to read [and] she's desperate to get onto chapter books'. This strongly suggests that 'learning to read' was indeed perceived as being symbolised by being 'on chapter books'. In terms of the books themselves, it can be assumed that these books were structured differently to the scheme books, and presumably were divided into chapters. However, Simona herself later confirmed that this was what she meant by the term 'black and white pages' when she stated, 'Yes ... yes ... I'm on chapter books – books with black and white pages'. Similarly, Imogen and Toby also seemed to believe that their success in reading was evidenced by 'being on chapter books'. For example, when asked if he was able to read during a second-phase interview, Toby's response was emphatic when he stated, 'Yes – I'm on chapter books'. Moreover, Imogen's Year 1 teacher reported that Imogen 'really wanted to get up to reading chapter books' when asked about her attitudes towards reading.

These findings help to clarify the children's perceptions of the role reading scheme texts play in the journey towards becoming 'a reader'. If being 'a reader' means that you have achieved the status of being put 'on chapter books', then the reading scheme could be perceived as having a role in the attainment of this position. Many of the other children in this study also seemed to believe that reading scheme books *teach* reading, while non-reading scheme books can be read once a child has reached a level of competency, and has therefore *learned* to read. This was illustrated in the Book-bag activity when Imogen was asked to say which book she thought was Charlie Chick's favourite. In response, Imogen pointed to the reading scheme book stating, 'these because they're easier to read and they're good to understand, than the bigger books'. Yet she went on to report that Charlie Chick's teacher and parents would want him to be able to read the story books and the non-fiction books, because this would mean 'that he'd learned more from them'. When asked why the teacher did not give these books to the children to put in their book-bags, Imogen replied that 'teachers know that we won't be able to read these, so there's no point in having them'.

This suggests that Imogen views the reading scheme as a series of stepping stones that teach children how to read, so they are then able to access 'other' books in the future. In other words, given that Imogen herself was 'on chapter books', she seemed to be claiming that teachers and parents want children to be able to read non-scheme books because this would indicate that they had learned to read. However, until this time came, there was 'no point' in children attempting to read non-scheme books because they would be too difficult, hence her suggestion that Charlie Chick would want to read the scheme book because 'they're good to understand'. This was further evident when Imogen was told that Charlie Chick can read some of the words in his reading scheme book, but not all, and asked if she thought he was 'a reader'. She replied, 'He can read, yes, but he's not one of the advanced readers'. She then explained that she herself had been 'on Stage 9' which she found 'really easy', so she was 'moved onto chapter books'. This again confirms that Imogen regards reading as a progressive process that is measured according to the level of reading scheme text ascribed to an individual child.

These findings provide strong evidence to support Solity and Vousden's claim that reading scheme systems can promote the belief that the primary goal of reading is to 'get through the reading scheme and become a "free reader"' rather then learning to enjoy reading (2009: 502). For many children in The Oakfield Study, this did appear to be very much the case, though there was evidence to suggest that 'being on chapter books' was not desirable simply due to issues of perceived status in reading. Having stated that Imogen wanted to 'get up to reading chapter books', Imogen's teacher then reported that this was partly because Imogen wanted 'to be able to choose what she wanted to read'. As a consequence of this, it was further reported that Imogen would often now choose to read a book in the book corner when given an opportunity to choose activities freely within the classroom. Therefore, Imogen appears to genuinely enjoy the liberation of being 'on chapter books' and, like Simona, articulated a sense of frustration with the constraining elements associated with the *process* of learning to read.

This section has shown how young children's perceptions of themselves as readers can be heavily influenced by the use of reading scheme systems. What is more, attainment in reading was not only judged on the basis of place within the scheme, but actually determined whether the children viewed themselves as readers or not. Interestingly, this was exactly the criticism made of reading schemes over three decades ago. For example, Smith (1973; 1978) argued that reading schemes can be damaging for children because they change the 'nature' of reading from comprehension and appreciation of text to the memorisation of phonic rule. Yet it must be pointed out that the three children discussed in this section were not only from the Reception cohort, but all perceived themselves as confident and able readers. What is more, all had successfully worked their way through the system and were 'enjoying a sense of liberty from the constraints of the school-based learning process' (Levy, 2009b: 373). But what are the implications of this for children who are less confident in their abilities as readers? Is it possible that perceptions of the role reading schemes play in determining proficiency can cause discouragement for some children? This appears to be very much the case.

Reading schemes: discouraging reading

Given that young children spend a considerable amount of their time, both at home and at school, engaged in the reading of scheme texts, it seems important that educators understand how this reading is perceived. The above discussion highlighted that the reading of scheme texts was very much viewed by the children as 'training' in reading.

Through the medium of the reading scheme, young children believed that they were learning to read so that they could eventually access texts existing outside of the scheme. This of course raises many questions with regard to children's attitudes and perceptions of reading, but the first pertains to the actual reading of the texts themselves and the extent to which the children viewed this reading as authentic.

Like many of the other children in the study, Joseph seemed to equate concepts of 'reading' with an ability to read his reading scheme books. For example, when asked to tell Charlie Chick what reading was, Joseph replied with the question to Charlie Chick, 'Have you ever read any Floppy books once?' Yet it appeared that Joseph did not regard this reading as being 'real'. One situation in which this was apparent occurred when he was asked if the children in the Small World Play scenario could read. He replied, 'Not yet', but then reported that they would be able to read their 'book-bag books'. However Joseph went on to clarify that 'that's not real reading yet'. Consequently, Joseph seemed to regard reading scheme books as instrumental in teaching reading, but he did not view this process as authentic when situated within a wider definition of 'reading'. This perception was clarified further in the final stage of the study when Joseph was presented with a variety of books and asked which he thought were the most important. He pointed to the reading scheme books stating, 'These, because they help you learn. When you grow up you will be able to read them, and when you really really grow up, you will know how to read information books'.

It therefore appears that Joseph regards reading scheme books as a tool to teach reading, in much the same way as reported by many of the other children. Yet Joseph also seemed to believe that one must reach a level of competency within the reading scheme before an attempt could be made to read anything else. This was evident in the fact that he reported that the reading scheme would teach reading, so that when a child is 'really really grown up' he would be able to read information books. This perception was further confirmed when Joseph was asked if he could read the picture books on the table. To this he replied, 'No – but I can read these books', again pointing to the reading scheme book. While it has been previously identified that reading schemes do little to promote positive attitudes towards reading in lower-achieving pupils, Ofsted (2004) argued that this was because these children were often unable to read the books that they wanted to read, which reinforced feelings of incompetence. However, results from The Oakfield Study suggest that the structure of the reading scheme may in itself discourage children from reading, because they believe that they need to reach a level of competency within the scheme before owning the ability to read texts existing outside of the reading scheme.

Further evidence to suggest that this was the case could be found in Joseph's perceptions of the grading structure within the reading scheme. To illustrate, he was initially surprised, and impressed, to see that Charlie Chick had a 'Blue' book in his book-bag. Joseph explained that this meant that Charlie Chick was a 'Stage 3'. This impressed Joseph because, as Charlie Chick was regarded as a 'beginning' reader, Joseph reported that this meant that 'he's a good reader, because I started off on Book 1'. Moreover, during the home visit Joseph reported that he had 'nearly finished all the Book 4's [and was] nearly on Stage 5'. This again suggests that Joseph regards progress in reading as an ability to complete the various stages in his reading scheme. Yet this perception seemed to actively discourage him from wanting to look at other books, as he viewed himself as unable to read them.

The project data indicated that as Joseph progressed from Reception into Year 1, his relationship with books in general deteriorated. This was exemplified at the beginning of the third-stage interview when Joseph was presented with a variety of books in the Book-bag activity. His first reaction to this was to look very concerned and ask, 'Do I have to read these books?' which was clearly something that he did not want to do. What is more, later in the same interview when asked whether books would be 'better' placed at home or at school during the Home and School Reading activity, he replied, 'Nowhere! I hate that, so I've moved them away', while pushing the *Books* card across the table away from him. This is a particularly worrying issue, especially given that the 2006 Progress in International Reading Literacy Study (PIRLS) (Twist, Schagen and Hodgson, 2007) revealed that the attitudes of 10-year-old children in England towards reading are not only poor in comparison with children from other countries, but are also declining. It therefore seems crucial that we carefully consider how the teaching of reading influences children's attitudes towards reading. Certainly results from The Oakfield Study strongly suggest that the role of reading scheme texts must be carefully considered from the perspective of children's attitudes and confidences in reading as well as the 'mechanics' of reading instruction.

Joseph's profile revealed that he was indeed displaying negative attitudes towards reading by the time he was in Year 1 (aged 6), yet this was not the case for all the children. In fact Annie's self-confidence in reading appeared to grow in between the first and second phases of the study. For example, having reported that learning to read words in books was 'hard' during the Reception Charlie Chick interview, she reported that this was now 'easy' during the second-phase interview. What is more, classroom observations of an independent reading activity and a guided reading session revealed that she appeared to enjoy both activities and remained focused and engaged throughout. Yet despite this observed enjoyment of book-reading, like Joseph, Annie also appeared to believe that she had to be able to read all the books in her reading scheme before she was able to tackle any books outside of the scheme.

This was initially evident when Annie was asked to show Charlie Chick what reading was during the second phase of the study. Annie not only insisted upon selecting a reading scheme book, but was very concerned about having a book of the correctly assigned level. She reported, 'I will have to pick Stage 5 because I'm on Stage 5'. She then found a book which she initially believed to be a Stage 5 book (colour-coded orange) and began to try to read the words systematically on each page. Although this book was indeed from the Oxford Reading Tree, the book Annie had selected was a play and had not been levelled or colour-coded in the same way as the other books. Even though Annie was able to read much of the printed text with accuracy, her confidence soon became threatened when she realised that the format of the book was different to that of her general reading scheme books. She abruptly stopped reading and examined the back of the book stating that she thought this book was 'the wrong colour'. She then suggested that she should look for a Stage 4 book instead, stating, 'I can read Stage 4 – it's easy'.

The final phase of the study revealed that Annie continued to believe that her proficiency in reading was determined by the grade of her reading scheme book. What is more, it also became apparent in this phase that, like Joseph, Annie also believed that she could only read books from within her reading scheme. For example, when shown the range of books during the school-based interview, Annie reported, 'I can't read story books ...'cause they have little writing and I don't know what it is'. Moreover, she also reported that Charlie Chick would only be able to read the reading scheme book from the selection on display, stating that these were also his favourite books, 'because they've got nice pictures and some of them's got funny pictures'. She further reported that she thought Charlie Chick's teacher would prefer that he read the reading scheme books although she did also claim that the non-fiction books were the most 'important' because of subject content.

This suggests that Annie does enjoy reading her reading scheme books and is particularly fond of the illustrations within. However, it is also clear that she does not believe that she is capable of reading books outside of the reading scheme. As Annie also seemed to be concerned about her *level* in reading, as defined by the stage (or colour) of her current reading scheme book, it appears that Annie believes that she will not be a 'proper' reader until she has mastered all of the stages in her scheme, and has thus acquired the ability to read books outside of the reading scheme. This is clearly a cause for concern as it has been documented that for lower-achieving pupils, the struggle to work through the reading scheme can result in feelings of failure and the attitude that reading is 'simply ... a chore' (Solity and Vousden, 2009: 474).

Yet The Oakfield Study further revealed that as well as being a 'chore', the reading scheme actually discouraged some children from reading. As Annie and Joseph approached the end of Year 1, they both regarded themselves as unable to read books existing outside of the reading scheme. Consequently, little attempt was made by either child to read even the most basic of picture book texts independently, as they seemed to believe that they did not have the necessary capabilities to do so. In other words, a lower position within the reading scheme appeared to constrain any attempt to read beyond the scheme, as it promoted a perceived lack of proficiency in reading and therefore an inability to read books outside of the scheme. What is more, even children who regarded themselves as successful readers, such as Toby and Imogen, appeared to share this belief. However, in contrast to Annie and Joseph, Toby and Imogen saw themselves as successful largely because they had completed the progression through the stages of the reading scheme and were therefore liberated from such constraints.

But what does this mean for children who are just beginning their Reception year? How do such concepts affect their perceptions of themselves as readers? To return now to the original Nursery cohort, the cases of Huda and Ibrihim illuminate how these same issues influenced their own perceptions of themselves as readers and their attitude towards books over the course of their Reception year. Data gathered during the first phase of the study suggested that Huda largely regarded reading in positive terms. Though she did categorise the cards *Learning to read words in books* and *Learning to read words on the computer* as 'hard' during the Learning Skills activities in both Phases 1 and 2, further data gathered during the Nursery year suggested that she did view herself as able to read because reading was perceived as synonymous with simply enjoying books. Yet data collected during the second phase of the study indicated that Huda had become less positive about reading and indeed the process of learning to read. This appeared related to the fact that

Huda now not only believed that reading was defined as an ability to read books from within the reading scheme, but that this reading needed to be fluent.

This was suggested on a number of occasions, especially in relation to Huda's perceptions of reading behaviours. For example, when asked to tell Charlie Chick what reading is, Huda elected to *demonstrate* reading by pretending to read words from an imaginary book. When then asked if she could actually show Charlie Chick what reading is, Huda looked at the picture books on the table and replied, 'I don't know how to read this book'. Yet when asked if she could read a reading scheme book, she replied 'Yes'. Huda then selected a reading scheme book and invented her own words to accompany the pictures. One can only speculate as to why Huda felt she could invent her own words for the scheme book, but not the picture book, but it does seem possible that Huda selected the scheme book to demonstrate reading not because she was able to decode the print within this book but because she felt she *ought* to be reading the scheme book. In other words, it seems likely that Huda now saw reading as the requirement to learn to read reading scheme books. This again supports Smith's (1973; 1978) original argument that reading schemes can define the nature of reading and thus shape children's definitions of reading and being 'a reader'.

What is more, it seemed that Huda regarded authentic readers as those able to read texts with fluency, yet she also appeared frustrated by her own inability to do this. For example, when given the opportunity to choose freely from the books in the classroom, Huda did not appear to have an interest in any of the books available and returned to her seat empty-handed. She then asked her teacher for a particular book and the teacher responded by asking the whole class if anyone has the 'teeny book on hedgehogs in winter' because Huda had requested to look at it. The book was then quickly raised by another girl who happily handed it to Huda.

Yet when Huda took the book to her table she made no attempt to look at either the printed text or the pictures, choosing instead to simulate what can be described as almost a caricature of fluent 'reading behaviour'. She put her face close inside the book (where she clearly would be unable to focus on any element of the text) and created the sounds 'dobo duboy dobo duboy'. Recognising that this was an attempt to simulate reading, another child close to Huda then retorted, 'That's not proper reading!' This comment did not seem to concern Huda who continued to simulate this reading behaviour for a further few minutes before quickly losing interest in the book. After a considerable delay, Huda then selected a second book. Her behaviour with this book is documented in these observation field notes:

> Huda picks up the book, saying 'Blah, blah, blah' as she turns the pages. Her gaze appears to be on the print as she does this, as if she is simulating print reading. She soon becomes distracted, holding the book high above her head and wobbling it from side to side. She then brings the book back to the table. For a brief moment she seems to become focused on a picture, but then quickly loses interest as she begins looking around the room.

It therefore appears that the interest Huda showed in books during Nursery may not initially have transferred into Reception. This could possibly be connected to the fact that her perceptions of what was meant by the terms 'reading' and 'learning to read' changed from regarding reading as the simple enjoyment of books to the need to decode printed text with fluency. What is more, as Huda had been assigned to the lowest reading group in the class it also seemed very likely that she no longer regarded herself as able to read, as defined by this new 'schooled' definition of 'reading'.

Further evidence to suggest that this was indeed the case could be found in the final stage of data collected. By the end of the Reception year, Huda appeared to have regained a more positive attitude towards reading and the use of books. This seemed to be linked to the fact that Huda was now experiencing far more success in decoding print within her reading scheme books. Her teacher reported that 'she's done so well' and as a result has moved up into 'a different reading group'. She went on to explain that her sight vocabulary had improved greatly over the last two months, stating, 'in March she knew only nine [of the 44 Reception sight-vocabulary words] but now, only two months later, she knew 34'. Moreover, Huda's teacher also reported that Huda did not 'know the sounds' of letters and letter blends when she first came into Reception, but now has a knowledge of 'basically all the sounds' which she uses to do 'real reading'.

However, even though Huda now appeared to regard herself as a reader, she seemed to very much link this perception with the ability to read reading scheme books. For example, when asked in the Phase 3 school-based interview if she could read she replied, 'Yes – I can read those [pointing to the Oxford Reading Tree books on the table]'. Moreover, when shown Charlie Chick's reading scheme book in his book-bag,

Huda spontaneously asked, 'Shall I read it to him?' which again suggested a confidence in reading these scheme books. She also went on to report that 'the words are easy [in] the Kipper books' although she did state that she did not know all of the words in these books. All in all, this suggests that Huda has found a certain confidence with her reading scheme books. However, this confidence did not seem to extend towards other books outside of the reading scheme.

When asked to look at the display of books on the table during the Book-bag activity, Huda's immediate response was filled with concern as she stated, 'I don't know how to read those'. When asked if she thought these books were 'harder' than the reading scheme books, Huda provided an affirmative response. Moreover, when asked which books she thought her teacher would want her to read, Huda replied, 'Kipper books ... because you choose one and you read it'. This again suggests that reading scheme books are regarded as not only manageable, in terms of her being able to read them, but also essential within the process of learning to read. Further evidence for this was found when Huda was told that Charlie Chick's friend was able to read picture books but could not read reading scheme books and asked if that meant he was a reader. Huda reported that this meant that Charlie Chick's friend was 'not a reader', thus confirming her belief that one has to be able to progress through the process of reading scheme books in order to be defined as 'a reader'.

As observed in the responses of the Reception children, Huda also appeared to regard books outside of the reading scheme as 'too hard' to read. However, her comments differed from those of the Reception children in that she appeared to believe that being 'a reader' was sig-nalled by an ability to read reading scheme books, rather than these books serving as training for the 'real' reading that will occur outside of the reading scheme. It therefore seems possible that not only are these non-scheme books regarded as 'hard' to read, but that there was little motivation for Huda to read them as she believed that she was expected to learn to read scheme material first.

Like Huda, Ibrihim also appeared to believe that reading had much to do with the decoding of words, especially within the context of reading scheme books. When presented with the display of picture books in the second-phase interview and asked to show Charlie Chick what reading was, he too responded by saying, 'I don't know how to read these books', before asking, 'Which ones are easy?' Like many of the other children in this study, Ibrihim also appeared to believe that he was unable to read picture books. Yet when shown Charlie Chick's book-bag in the final-phase interview, Ibrihim became very excited when he saw the reading scheme book, shouting, 'I can read that'.

Throughout this final-phase interview, Ibrihim continued to select and ask to read other books from the Oxford Reading Tree scheme, which suggested that he may in fact have been enjoying reading these books. While it seems likely that Ibrihim did enjoy reading the Oxford Reading Tree books, it also appears that he enjoyed seeing himself progress through the stages in the reading scheme. This was brought to light when his mother reported that he always changes his book every day without prompting and enjoys reading the books to her at home. Ibrihim's mother then explained that Ibrihim liked to write the title of his book in his reading diary every night by himself. The suggestion that Ibrihim therefore enjoyed seeing himself progress through the different books in his scheme was later confirmed by his teacher who also commented that Ibrihim 'wants to progress'. Ibrihim's teacher went on to report that 'he doesn't particularly repeat books because he knows he can read those books'. These comments all suggest that Ibrihim does get a sense of achievement from seeing himself progress from one book to another within the reading scheme and seemed to like having his progress documented in his reading diary.

This raises the issue of purpose once again. It may well have been the case that Ibrihim was enjoying reading his scheme books, but it also seems possible that he perceived the goal of reading 'as being to get through the reading scheme … rather than being to derive meaning and enjoyment from what is read' (Solity and Vousden, 2009: 502). What is more, these findings strongly indicated that although these issues may have had a particular salience for children who had poorer perceptions of themselves as readers, the role of reading scheme texts has huge relevance for all children learning to read in schools today.

☐ Summary

This chapter has examined the ways in which children view and value book texts and perceive them in terms of affordance. Furthermore, this chapter has also described how these perceived affordances can influence young children's perceptions of themselves as readers. Results from The Oakfield Study have revealed that children as young as 4 or 5 years of age may already be beginning to form

(Continued)

(Continued)

sophisticated constructions of what it means to be a reader. As these cases have shown, it appears that the school context is largely responsible for shaping definitions of reading. In particular it is clear that the ways in which reading scheme texts are perceived can have a particularly profound effect upon children's self-perceptions of reading as well as their wider relationships with books.

Findings from The Oakfield Study indicated that many of the children perceived success in reading as strongly related to achievement within their reading scheme. What is more, it was widely believed that reading scheme books exist so as to *teach* reading, whereas non-scheme books were not regarded as having a role in either the teaching or learning of reading. For many of the Reception cohort in particular, this meant that they did not perceive themselves as actual 'readers' until they had completed all the stages in the scheme and had thus been awarded the position of being 'on chapter books'. For those children in this study who had reached the stage of being on chapter books, this initiated a sense of liberation from the constraints of the system, almost as if permission had been granted for them to read books outside of the reading scheme.

For others who were still operating within the levels of the reading scheme, the effect of this perception was disturbing. As these children did not regard the reading of their scheme books as authentic reading, they appeared to make little attempt to read books that extended beyond the reading scheme. Even picture books with very little print content were regarded as being 'too hard' to read, until they had achieved a certain proficiency in reading as dictated by the grading system operational in the classroom. In this respect the stringent use of reading scheme books in Reception could be seen to actively discourage children from reading and further enhance the negative perceptions children may have of themselves as readers.

This has substantial implications for the teaching of reading in early years settings. This chapter has raised serious concerns about the ways in which a dominant use of reading scheme systems can shape what 'counts' (Luke, Carrington and Kapitzke, 2003: 252) as reading literacy in school settings. Though it is clear that children do need to learn how to use phonics, this chapter gives strong evidence to suggest that by defining reading in this way, reading schemes do little to promote meaningful engagement with texts. Further, as UKLA (2006, 3.23) stress, 'phonics is necessary'. However, they urge educators to 'keep the end in mind' and recognise that the goal of reading instruction is 'to develop effective and enthusiastic readers'.

This is a particularly crucial issue, given the current direction that curriculum policy into the teaching of reading is following. The National Literacy Strategy (NLS) (DfEE, 1998) proposed that children essentially used four potential decoding strategies (searchlights): knowledge of phonics, word recognition, grammar and context. Yet the Rose Review (Rose, 2006) into the teaching of early reading in England recommended that the 'searchlights model' of reading should be replaced by the 'Simple View of Reading' (SVR) (see Appendix 1 of the Rose Review, 2006). As Kirby and Savage (2008) identify, the SVR advocates that reading comprehension (RC) is the product of listening comprehension (LC) and decoding (D); thus $RC = LC \times D$ (Kirby and Savage, 2008: 75). Yet having defended this recommendation Stuart et al. argue that 'sight word recognition and phonic decoding must take precedence to ensure reading fluency, the first step to successful text comprehension' (2008: 61). As a consequence, the Primary National Strategy (PNS) has now 'rejected the searchlights model and recommended phonics as the first and most useful decoding skill for beginning readers' (Solity and Vousden, 2009: 471).

Given the issues raised in this chapter, it seems crucial that educators and policy makers give careful consideration to the ways in which texts are allowed to define what is meant by the term 'reading' and the implications this has for young children's developing perceptions of themselves as readers. In particular, teachers are encouraged to consider the following questions in relation to the use of book texts in the classroom.

Key questions

- What can be learned from young children's beliefs about the affordances of book texts? What are the implications of this for classroom practice?
- How can teachers ensure that reading scheme texts are not allowed to define goals in reading and the perceived status of young children as readers?
- How can texts be used more usefully to encourage confidence in reading and develop positive self-perceptions?
- What are the alternatives to graded reading systems?

5

Reading in multidimensional forms

Chapter Overview

The previous chapter described how book texts can play a crucial role in shaping how young children come to develop understandings of what it means to be a reader. However, as discussed in Chapter 1, children's textual world is currently changing, particularly in the light of technological advancement. As children enter the schooling system, the chances are that they will already have accumulated much experience in handling and making meaning from a wide variety of different texts. These texts may include environmental print and image such as those seen on supermarket logos and car badge symbols, as well as texts associated with digital media and popular culture. Indeed, the reading experience of the modern child extends far and beyond those of paper-based origins, yet the implications of this multidimensional reading for the schooling of reading is not yet well understood. This chapter therefore explores how the reading of multidimensional texts can have an impact on children's attitudes and motivations for reading and influence their perceptions of themselves as readers. In particular, the role of screen reading is discussed, with an emphasis on the ways in which children use computer technology. However, the crucial question to consider relates to the implications this all has for the teaching and learning of reading in schools.

In order to examine these implications, there are several questions that need to be considered. It has been argued that definitions of reading must broaden in order to accommodate the 'new textual landscapes'

(Carrington, 2005) of modern communication systems (Kress, 1997). For example, Bearne argues that we 'need to redefine what "literacy" involves [and] … note new uses of the term "text"' (2004: 16). But what impact would such a redefinition have on the ways in which children are taught to read today? Researchers have indeed documented concern that the reading of multidimensional texts, which are so familiar to many children in today's society, goes unrecognised in the literacy curriculum and its assessment (Bearne, 2003; 2004; Marsh, 2003b; Pahl, 2002). More specifically Burnett (2010) notes that the 'Early Learning Goals' for 'Communication, Language and Literacy' (Department for Education, 2010), which determine expectations for children's achievement by the age of 5, 'contain no reference to children's engagement with digital texts'. So how should the schooling of reading reflect the digital age in which young readers are growing up? And what can we learn from the ways in which children interact with multidimensional texts to inform the current reading curriculum?

These questions require that we look broadly at the ways in which the digital age is influencing how children today develop skills to become readers of text. This is discussed in the opening sections of this chapter, beginning with a reflection on the ways in which aspects of digital literacy penetrate children's reading today. However, there is no denying that children do need to develop specific skills in print literacy in order to be able to read many texts. This brings us to the second issue for discussion in this chapter. As Marsh and Singleton point out, there is now a substantial body of research that has been driven by a concern to understand 'how technology can enhance learners' skills, knowledge and understanding in relation to the reading and writing of print' (2009: 1). Recognising these concerns, and that there is indeed an expectation that children learn to read print during their early years in school, questions concerning the ways in which multidimensional texts influence children's perceptions of print literacy are raised and discussed towards the latter half of this chapter.

Digital literacy

There is much research to suggest that young children entering the formal education system today are already experienced in handling a variety of digital media. Marsh et al. found that 'young children are immersed in practices relating to popular culture, media and new technologies from birth' (2005: 5) and that parents are generally positive about the role of such media in their children's lives. Moreover, Bearne et al.

discovered that young children show 'expertise' in on-screen reading 'even where homes have no computers' (2007: 11), because the handling of such texts is now part of a culturally accepted discourse. It has therefore been argued that young children are developing the skills to become 'digitally literate' (Glister, 1997) from their earliest years of life. But what does this term actually mean?

The literature offers several definitions. However, the term does seem to acknowledge that young children are developing strategies that allow them to access and read a variety of digital texts with fluency and that these skills can be transferred from one digital context to another. This was especially apparent in the cases of Shaun (Nursery) and Joseph (Reception) in The Oakfield Study, both of whom had little opportunity to use computer technology in their own homes, but had clearly developed the digital skills needed to use computers through their interactions with other aspects of multimedia.

Although Shaun's family did own a computer, it was reported that it was used only 'occasionally' because it did not work very well. As a result, Shaun's engagement with interactive technology in the home was confined largely to game play on the television (interactive games on Sky), small hand-held games consoles and the mobile phone. Yet Shaun demonstrated a remarkable ability to use the computer with confidence and skill in the Nursery setting. For example, Shaun's teacher reported that Shaun will 'spend ages on some games' and 'can do loads on the computer' despite having received very little instruction in how to use the computer within the school context. What is more, during the Small World Play activity, Shaun not only showed a great deal of interest in the computer artefacts, but demonstrated that he possessed a great deal of technical knowledge and could use vocabulary associated with computers. For example, he reported that 'you press these buttons to play games and stuff', spoke of using 'the mouse', referred to terms such as 'website' and 'DVD', and explained the function of the cursor. It therefore appeared that although Shaun's exposure to the computer in his home environment had been minimal, he had developed a certain digital literacy through his interaction with other multimedia, which was transferred into the school setting and applied to the context of the computer.

While Merchant appears to agree that the term 'digital literacy' can be used to describe the ways in which children access media texts, he argues that it relates to more than a confidence in handling screen texts and should be orientated towards the 'study of written or symbolic representation that is mediated by new technology' (2007: 121). Marsh further argues that while digital literacy practices can be reflected in the more traditional aspects of literacy practice, there are 'distinct aspects of text analysis and production using new media' (2005: 5) that relate specifically to the use of digital texts. In other words, both Marsh and Merchant appear to be suggesting that the term 'digital literacy' implies that there is much to be understood about the ways in which young children learn to read digital texts, and decode the symbolic systems within, to further our understanding of how children become readers of text today. Given that young children do indeed appear to be entrenched in the communicative practices of multimedia (Kress and van Leeuwen, 2001) even before they begin formal schooling, this has clear implications for the teaching and learning of literacy in the early years classroom. This chapter now examines how young children learn to read multidimensional texts and the implications this has for classroom practice, beginning with a reflection on the use of computer technology.

Using computers at home and at school

Considering the many changes that have occurred in children's reading experiences over the last two decades, the role of the computer is perhaps one of the most important factors to consider. As raised earlier, while it appears that young children are developing skills in handling computer texts even when they do not have access to computers in their own homes (Bearne et al., 2007; Levy, 2009a), it has also been acknowledged that the impact of computers in children's lives is largely dependent on the social structures that are in place within children's homes (Facer et al., 2003; Holloway and Valentine, 2003).

This was perhaps especially evident among the Nursery cohort of children in The Oakfield Study. Although the Nursery teacher reported that all of the children in her class liked using the computer, Shaun was the only child from the sample reported to have a particular enthusiasm for the computer. The teacher reported that Huda did 'not use the computer loads', and that Kelly 'doesn't play on it much' either, while Ibrihim was described as not having much of an interest in the computer at all. Yet the mothers of all three of these children described their children as having a real enthusiasm for the computer and spoke of being impressed by their children's abilities to use the computer unaided in their homes. This not only suggests that these children became proficient in using the computer in their homes but also that their competencies were not recognised in the school system.

This does not mean, however, that children's responses to computer texts are in some ways homogeneous. Indeed Bennett et al. (2008) have argued that we need to be cautious about assuming that young children are 'digital natives' (Barlow, 1996; Tapscott, 2009) and therefore all tend to develop specific abilities in the handling of computer and digital texts. Findings from The Oakfield Study support Bennett's assertion, suggesting that confidences and attitudes towards computer technology were highly individual. However, the study further implied that we still have much to learn about the ways in which young children develop skills in reading computer texts.

Reading computer texts

Findings from The Oakfield Study revealed that most of the children in this study were using a wide variety of multimodal cues to make meaning from computer texts. The children were often observed using picture, sound, symbol, colour and print as they navigated the texts. Yet rather than viewing these cues in isolation from each other, the children appeared to tackle computer texts in a 'holistic' fashion, using the cues simultaneously to make meaning from the text.

To illustrate, it was clear that most of the children understood the meaning of many symbols on the computer, though they each used different language to describe what the symbols meant. For example, it was evident that the 'e' symbol for Internet Explorer had meaning for Huda, who reported that the sign 'means *CBeebies*' which she explained 'have lots of games there – and puzzles'. Similarly, Kelly reported that she recognised the 'e' symbol as being 'on my computer'. Moreover, Simona reported that the timer symbol 'means you have to wait', while Joseph stated that the same symbol meant 'don't touch it'. Finally, many of the children in the study were also observed spontaneously clicking on the English Flag symbol when entering a program, although they did not all know what the symbol stood for. For example, Malcolm reported that the symbol was something that 'helps it to load up'. In fact, this particular icon allowed the participant to access the game in English. However, Malcolm had realised that this icon needed to be clicked in order for his game to load.

These examples illustrate the ways in which the young children in this study were making meaning from pictorial images and icons within the context of computer screen texts. What is more, as the next section reveals, these children also appeared to be handling printed prompts on screen in much the same way as they were using iconic symbols. In other words, the children appeared to be embedding print reading within a broader and more 'holistic' approach to reading when using computer texts. This suggests that there is a need to consider the ways in which the reading of screen texts differs from that of paper-based media and what this means for young children learning to read today. Indeed Bearne et al. concluded their own investigation into children's screen reading with the recommendation that there is a 'need for more, and more detailed research into young children's use of screens' (2007: 29), particularly in relation to the interpretation of words, symbols and icons.

Certainly, it does appear to be very much the case that those involved in the education of young children today do need to gain a deeper understanding of the ways in which children learn to read on screen and the implications this has for the reading of all texts, whether of screen or paper-based origin. As so far revealed, it seems likely that many young children not only develop motivations and enthusiasm for computer texts, but are acquiring a breadth of skill through their interactions with technology that allows them to read a variety of digital texts with relative ease. However, as discussed in the previous chapter, structured aspects of print literacy continue to 'take precedence' (Stuart et al., 2008: 61) in defining what is meant by the term 'reading' in schools. With this in mind, the next section looks a little more closely at the issue of print reading on screen and how this fits into the acquisition of digital literacy skill.

Responding to print on screen

As the previous section explained, the children in The Oakfield Study were observed using iconic pictures and symbols to abstract meaning from computers, yet it was apparent that many of the children were also using print in much the same way as they used pictorial symbols. For example, when Ibrihim was showing Charlie Chick how to use the computer he came upon the two printed options *Play* and *Exit* when attempting to load a game. Despite the fact that Ibrihim did not appear to know what the words said, he confidently selected the *Play* option. When asked how he knew to click on this option he replied 'I just know'. When then asked what would have happened if he had chosen the other option he responded, 'It stops'. This indicates that even though Ibrihim could not decode the print as such, he understood the meaning of the words in this context, and was able to use the printed prompts to access his game.

Similarly, Caitlyn was faced with the words, 'The end. Do you want to see your story again?', once she had created her story in the *Humpty Dumpty* computer game. Given that Caitlyn had never played this game before, and that there were no other auditory or visual cues available to help her to extract meaning from this text, it was noteworthy that she too appeared to have an understanding of what the print meant. When asked what she thought the words said, she replied, 'When you click on this one, you make it come on again'. Although Caitlyn was unable to decode any of the printed words, she obviously had a strong sense of what the words could reasonably say in this context and was therefore able to abstract meaning from them.

This suggests that these children were using their broader knowledge of how computer texts work in order to make meaning from print as well as iconic symbols. In other words, they showed an ability to utilise their digital 'funds of knowledge' (Moll et al., 1992) or their broader 'digital literacy' (Glister, 1997) skills when attempting to make sense of print in these texts. This was shown repeatedly in The Oakfield Study, where many of the children consistently revealed that they understood the meaning of printed prompts on screen, though they were unable to decode the print. For example, the options *Play* or *Play Again* were reported to be 'Start' or 'Go'. The *Home* prompt was often recognised by the children and reported to mean 'Back' or 'Stop'. Finally, many of the children were observed clicking on the *Games* prompt, which appeared regularly on screen especially during the Computer-assisted activity. Once again, even though it was rare that a child could decode this print, many of the children seemed to have learned that this icon (even in an unfamiliar text) would lead them into a games page.

While there is a growing body of research that is attempting to investigate how technology can be used in specific ways to support children's phonological development (Comaskey et al., 2009) and skills in reading comprehension (Yuill et al., 2009), results from The Oakfield Study indicate that there is much to be gained from deepening our understanding of the ways in which children's own general interactions with technology, and perhaps computer technology in particular, can help them to develop confidence and skill in handling print. This issue is particularly salient given that the previous chapter identified that some young children may be losing confidence in reading print from their earliest years in school, as they believe that they are unable to meet the expectations of the school discourse. It therefore stands to reason that we acknowledge the ways in which screen texts can be more usefully used within the school context in order to promote confidence in reading.

One particular strategy that was identified in The Oakfield Study concerned children's use of 'trial and error' techniques when attempting to use print on screen. For example, having decided that he wanted to play the *Humpty Dumpty* game in the first phase of the study, it was clear that Malcolm knew that he needed to click on an icon from the desktop in order to access the game, but did not know which one to choose. He then employed a 'trial and error' technique, clicking on different printed prompts, then working his way back to the desktop when he realised that his attempt to access the game had been unsuccessful. Yet Malcolm did not appear concerned by these failed attempts; on the contrary he seemed very engaged with the process and was keen to keep trying out new options, saying, 'I know [laughs] maybe you have to try ... something else. Maybe that one isn't really our – maybe we need a video or something'. When Malcolm eventually found the menu to the *Humpty Dumpty* game he became very excited and was clearly proud of his accomplishment. Indeed Malcolm was by no means alone in using this strategy when faced with unfamiliar print. Huda, Caitlyn and Joseph were all observed employing similar 'trial and error' strategies in the handling of unfamiliar print and all appeared comfortable in using these self-regulatory (Horner and O'Conner, 2007) techniques.

It is noteworthy that Bearne et al. (2007: 25) also discovered that older children were using 'trial and error' strategies when attempting to navigate particular sites on the internet. They concluded that the use of these techniques indicated 'a lot of perseverance' but also a lack of skill in being able to select appropriate sites and locate information within these sites. This suggests that the medium of the computer may allow children to use print in a way that differs from paper-based texts. The application of 'trial and error' techniques indicates that, for some children at least, the computer may provide territory for them to 'try out' aspects of printed text use without fear of 'getting it wrong' or making mistakes. This contrasts somewhat with the issues raised in the previous chapter, which indicated that many young children are extremely inhibited about the presence of print in books and believe that it must be rigorously and accurately decoded in order to meet the demands of the school system. However, Bearne et al.'s work does further suggest that there is a need for schools to include more active teaching in the use of multimodal texts in the curriculum in order to help children to benefit more fully from what these texts have to offer.

This chapter has so far identified that many young children are developing skills in reading digital and screen texts even before entry into the formal education system. It has been argued that computer texts may have a particular role to play in promoting children's ability to handle various sign and symbol systems, as well as developing strategies to tackle text in general with confidence. As this section has highlighted, issues of confidence in using print seem especially relevant to the use of multimodal texts and therefore deserve further exploration. Bearing in mind Marsh and Singleton's assertion that there is a need to understand how aspects of technology can 'enhance learners' skills, knowledge and understanding in relation to the reading and writing of print' (2009: 1), the next section looks more closely at the relationship between print reading on screen and within paper-based contexts, and the implications this has for the teaching of reading today.

Reading print on paper and screen

Chapter 1 opened with a description of four documented perspectives on learning to read. While it was stressed that the cognitive-psychological approach, with its emphasis on the decoding of print, was never divorced from other teaching methods, there was an 'age' in which it dominated the teaching of reading. In her article 'The four ages of reading philosophy and pedagogy', Turbill (2002: 3) speaks of a period from about the 1950s into the early 70s as 'the age of reading as decoding'. She describes this age as a time when it was believed that if children were taught 'how to decode the print, comprehension … would follow'. While Turbill goes on to state that this approach to the teaching and learning of reading 'served the cultural age in which it operated', she argues that 'we cannot teach reading this way in our current age'. Recognising the impact of new digital technologies within children's reading diets, Turbill argues that learning to read is a 'far more complex process in the '00s' than ever before and urges schools to accept the plurality of literacy in modern society.

As evidenced throughout this book, definitions of 'reading' should now acknowledge the wide range of multimedia and modes available to children today. However, this raises questions about the role of print literacy within such a definition as well as questions pertaining to the ways in which teachers need to consider teaching children to read print. This concept was explored by Hassett (2006) who challenged the use of traditional alphabetic print literacy by suggesting that constructions of early reading instruction need to be reframed within a context of new technologies and changing textual structure. She argues that the early literacy curriculum and its assessment maintains a particular and permanent notion of literacy that 'is tied tightly to alphabetic print concepts' (2006: 82). She goes on to stress that as a consequence, a reluctance for education to accept new forms of reading has less to do 'with a "new" medium' and more to do with 'the way that alphabetic print literacy discourses are maintained in education'.

Hassett is therefore arguing that early years educators need to recognise that children find meaning in the signs and symbols of texts that go beyond the traditional characteristics of alphabetic print and that print-literacy skills need to become embedded within a broader discourse on reading which values all sign and symbol systems. Findings from The Oakfield Study strongly support this assertion, given that the young children in this study appeared to be making sense of print on screen in much the same way as they were decoding pictures and visual images. What is more, this appeared to help some children develop confidence in their abilities to handle print. As discussed earlier, many of the children in this study appeared more comfortable using print within the context of the computer, in comparison with paper-based texts, as this medium did not seem to carry the same requirements to decode.

This was illustrated particularly well in Joseph's profile. Joseph consistently reported, during the first phase of the study, that it was easier to read words on computers than in books. When asked why this was the case he replied, 'Because books have lots of words and computers doesn't'. What is more, having reported in the Small World Play activity that the girl looking at the book would find it 'hard' to read, while the same girl would find it 'easy' to read from the computer, he went on to explain that it is easier to read and write words on the computer because 'you can hear them in your head'. Bearing in mind that Joseph does not have a particularly positive image of himself as a reader, this data suggests that Joseph does in fact feel less threatened by the presence of print on the computer, in comparison with books, partly because the computer has fewer words to read, but also because he finds that he can 'hear' the words more clearly within this context.

This again indicates that some children may regard the reading of print within the context of the computer as making different demands on the reader in comparison with book-based texts. Yet if children come to believe that print reading within book-based contexts is more important than reading on screen (as suggested in the previous chapter) then it seems possible that proficiency in screen reading could have little impact on children building positive perceptions of themselves as readers. Once again, The Oakfield Study strongly suggested that this was indeed the case.

During the first phase of the study, Caitlyn was observed confidently using print within computer texts, even though she was unable to decode it. Not only was Caitlyn observed doing this, but her mother also spoke of Caitlyn's ability to use computer texts unaided in the home. She reported, 'I don't know how she does it actually, because it has got writing in it'. However, by the second phase of the study Caitlyn was reporting that reading words on the computer was just as hard as reading words in books 'because it's the same as the computer, but it's just a different thing'. She further reported that it was also hard to write words on the computer because 'when you spell things you have to try and read them too'.

It is useful to reflect back at this point to Caitlyn's interactions with book texts, reported in Chapter 2. Caitlyn demonstrated a remarkable ability to create narratives of her own, using the pictures in books. However, as the study progressed, Caitlyn came to reject such strategies to make meaning from book texts, believing that this did not conform to a *correct* definition of reading as determined by the school discourse. In fact Caitlyn seemed to lose confidence in many of her own strategies to acquire meaning from texts as she became increasingly concerned that 'real' reading was about decoding print in books and seeing if 'the right letters' could be 'sounded out' – a strategy that she also described as being 'hard' and requiring a great deal of 'practice'. This therefore suggests that even though Caitlyn remained very positive about using computers throughout all three phases of the study, her anxieties about print reading in books appeared to intrude upon her interactions with print on screen also. This could possibly also explain why Caitlyn generally confined her screen reading to her home, as she felt it did not fit comfortably with the expectations of school.

This very much supports Turbill's (2002) and Hassett's (2006) assertions that the ways in which print literacy is taught in schools today need to be re-evaluated in the light of changing technologies. However, it does seem to be somewhat paradoxical that as children's experiences with text become increasingly multimodal, the teaching of reading seems to become more and more restricted, rooted in the belief that systematic phonic work 'offers the best route to becoming skilled readers' (Rose, 2006: 19). Yet as Caitlyn's case demonstrates, this reading discourse can actually prevent some young children from having the confidence to build upon their own strategies to make sense of print within the variety of contexts that are available to them today.

What is more, findings from The Oakfield Study indicated that Caitlyn was by no means alone in developing such inhibitions with print-based literacy on screen as well as in books. Malcolm was reported as having an interest and a competence in using the computer throughout all three stages of the study. Yet despite the fact that he was observed using picture and print together in his own reading of screen texts, he focused his attention on attempting to decode the print phonetically when showing Charlie Chick how to use a computer within the school context. By the final stage of the study, even though Malcolm's teacher reported that he 'is more confident with that [the computer]' than paper-based texts, it appeared that Malcolm's confidence in reading computer texts had also diminished. For example, having reported that the card demonstrating *Learning to read words on the computer* should receive a 'middle' rating in the Phase 2 Learning Skills activity, Malcolm categorised it as 'hard' in the final phase, while he continued to place the card *Learning to read words in books* in the 'middle' category. When asked why he thought it was harder to read words on the computer than in books, Malcolm's comments suggested that he was concerned that computers do not have a bank of key words, as one would expect to find in a school reading scheme. He reported, 'Books have certain words, and computers are a little bit hard and sometimes you have to sound them out'.

This suggests that Malcolm prefers to learn print by acquiring a 'sight vocabulary', rather than having to 'sound out' unfamiliar words phonetically. This concurs with his mother's comments, who reported that Malcolm 'knows certain key words like "the" and "is"' but would generally rely on picture cues to make sense of print. It therefore appears that Malcolm is highly dependent on his small bank of sight-read words in order to function as a perceived reader of text. While he evidently finds it hard to read his school scheme books, he appears to get some degree of security from the fact that they do 'have certain words' that he knows he can read, thus allowing him to operate as a reader, if only in a partial sense. As a consequence Malcolm appears to have become increasingly less confident in handling print on screen, as he does not seem to think that computers will help him build this bank of key vocabulary.

Like Caitlyn, although Malcolm had developed skills in reading computer texts, including aspects of print reading, he seemed to lose confidence in handling print within this context over the course of the study. Both children had found strategies of their own with which to make sense of print within the multimodal context of the computer, but as they progressed through their early years of schooling, they came to view print reading in more structured and isolated terms. In other words, conforming to the school discourse on reading, with its emphasis on the perceived need to decode print in books, was seen to threaten the children's own developing confidences in handling print.

However, Joseph's profile is perhaps the most worrying in this respect. As discussed at the beginning of this section, Joseph not only demonstrated a competence in using print within the context of the computer, he consistently reported a preference for reading print on screen, in comparison with book-based contexts, during the early phases of the study. Yet even though Joseph remained enthusiastic about using computers throughout the study, his confidence in reading print on screen was seen to decline. For example, having rated the card *Learning to read words on the computer* as 'easy' in the Learning Skills activity in Phase 1, this was reduced to a 'middle' rating in the second phase and was categorised as 'hard' in Phase 3. As Joseph consistently categorised *Learning to read words in books* as 'hard' throughout all three phases of the study, it appears that Joseph came to regard print reading on the computer as being just as difficult as print reading within paper-based contexts.

This is perhaps particularly relevant in view of the fact that Joseph seemed aware that the strategies he was using to make sense of print on the computer differed from those used to read print in books. He reported, for example, that you 'have to be able to understand words' to use the computer, but then later explained that this was different from reading words. This perception was further clarified when he stated that it was not necessary to be able to 'read words' on the computer, but claimed that people 'have to listen to words though, so you know what you are doing'. This suggests that Joseph believes that the multimodal nature of computer texts means that the reader does not have to actually decode print in these texts, as they can utilise other modes such as auditory representation. However, Joseph's profile, like the others discussed, suggests that he no longer values these strategies as contributing towards authentic 'reading' as defined by the school system.

This chapter has so far identified that digital texts can offer young children the opportunity to develop confidence in handling print. However, it has also warned that the domination of a narrow school discourse on print literacy can not only have a negative impact on children's interactions with book and paper texts, but can lead to reluctance to read print within screen contexts also. It must be recognised though that multimodal and multidimensional reading relates to more than computer technology. The next section looks briefly at children's print reading within a variety of multidimensional contexts.

Reading print in multidimensional forms

There is much evidence to suggest that the environment in which young children are immersed has a large role to play in shaping their early interactions with literacy. While studies have identified that the home environment is an important factor influencing children's literacy learning (Minns, 1997; Cairney, 2003), the degree of continuity between home and school literacy practices has also been recognised as a key factor (Heath, 1983; Tizard and Hughes, 1984; Levy, 2008). This issue is discussed in more detail in the following chapter. However, there is also a growing body of evidence indicating that early years educators can do much to promote positive literacy learning environments in early childhood settings (Makin, 2003: 334) by creating an environment that is 'positive, supportive and respectful'. It has been recognised that such environments are likely to be 'print rich' and afford children opportunities to experience print in a variety of contexts. However, there is also a strong call for educators to 'attempt to regain the high ground for play-based literacy learning' (Makin, 2003: 329) and acknowledge the importance of play within early literacy learning (Roskos and Christie, 2001).

The Oakfield Study supports these claims, suggesting that young children identify with printed images that are meaningful, and that schools need to find ways in which to capitalise on this in the creation of positive literacy learning environments. It was no surprise to find, as many others have undoubtedly found also, that several of the children showed a particular interest in print that was associated with their names. For example, Kelly's mother reported that Kelly enjoyed finding the letters from her name while eating alphabet potatoes, or spotting these letters on signs in the environment. Similarly, despite the fact that David appeared very hesitant around print during all school-based reading activities, he was observed becoming very excited when, during a reading activity, a teaching assistant held up a flashcard with the word 'Dad' on it. He cried out, 'Look – these two', pointing to the letters 'D' and 'a' before continuing, 'These two are in my name'. When it comes to issues of identity, there is clearly little more relevant to a child than their own name! Kelly also demonstrated that she could identify certain aspects of environmental print that were particularly relevant to her daily life. For example, her parents reported that she could recognise signs such as

'Sainsbury's', 'Asda' and 'Homebase', which were all shops situated near to her home. This again suggests that even the youngest of children may be 'tuning in' to aspects of print when the context is meaningful for them.

As these children were connecting aspects of print literacy to their own lives, the project data indicated that print literacy was included in the process of forming a literary identity. This was further evident in the Popular Culture activity, where children were asked to try to read and then match two corresponding sets of cards displaying print that appeared in standard and iconic forms (see Chapter 1). During this activity it became apparent that not only did all of the children recognise the iconic versions of the Popular Culture cards, many reported that they could identify the cards because they recognised them from their own everyday experiences. For example, many of the children claimed that they recognised certain cards because they had watched television programmes related to the icons (such as *CBeebies* or *Thomas the Tank Engine*). Joseph stated that he recognised *Barney* because 'that's on doors', while Simona reported that she knew *Thomas the Tank Engine* because 'I have books of it'. Annie, on the other hand, reported that she recognised *Scooby Doo* because 'I've got a Scooby Doo lunch box', while *Barbie* was reported to feature on the lunch box she had before.

Yet it appeared that these children were not just reading iconic symbols as a singular image, but were 'tuning in' to the print within the image. With the exception of David, all of the children demonstrated an increasing ability to match the printed Popular Culture card set to the corresponding iconic set over the course of the year, even in cases where the children were not print literate. This again demonstrates the importance of print being attached to a meaningful context if it is to appeal to younger children. Moreover, the project data provided further support for the argument that play is a vital feature in children's early literacy learning (Roskos and Christie, 2001). As the above examples illustrate, many of the children were indeed recognising elements of printed text from their engagement with popular culture in the form of play and interaction with television and multimedia texts. It has been well documented that popular culture and media texts play a crucial role in shaping children's literary identities and that further extensive analysis of such text use is needed so that early years educators can build on 'the extensive expertise' that children already have as consumers and producers of such texts (Marsh, 2005).

While this issue applied to all of the children in The Oakfield Study, it was perhaps especially apparent in David's case. As discussed in Chapter 2, despite showing very little interest in print both at home and at school, it was somewhat surprising to find that David was able to match all of the iconic Popular Culture cards to the standard printed set when he was in Nursery. This strongly suggested that through his own everyday interactions with popular culture and play, David was indeed making sense of printed images as well as pictorial symbols. However, when this activity was repeated during the second and third phases of the study, David was no longer able to match the cards. Although one can only speculate as to the reasons why this was the case, the project data does provide some highly plausible suggestions.

As highlighted in David's profile, he appeared to be one of the younger children in the class (though he was in fact one of the older). In comparison with the other Nursery children, he was probably the least interested in structured activity, but very much enjoyed engaging in superhero role play with his friends, which occupied most of his time during Nursery sessions. Given that researchers have identified a strong relationship between superhero play and literary identity (Marsh, 1999; 2000; Dyson, 1997), it very much appeared that superhero play provided fertile territory for David to create his own literary identity by affording opportunities for role play, communication, interaction with peers and engagement with text. However, once David moved into Reception, the daily routine became significantly more structured, affording him far less time to play. Not only did the teacher voice her concern that the structure of Reception did not serve David's best interests, but David was regularly observed looking lost and confused during structured activities.

The structure of the Nursery therefore appeared to provide David with opportunities to engage in symbolic play. Given that it has been identified that such play can contribute towards the development of reading as a holistic activity, whereby children learn through their own dialogic engagement with texts (Lysaker, 2006), it was clear that such interaction not only supported David's general developments in literacy, but also aided his specific understandings about print. Yet these understandings seemed to dissolve when David entered his Reception year. The imposition of a new discourse, which defined 'reading' primarily as the ability to decode printed words in books, not only had little meaning for David, but sent a clear message that he was not a successful reader.

☐ Summary

This chapter has identified a number of issues connected to young children's reading of multidimensional and multimodal texts. It has also highlighted the fact that many young children entering the schooling system today have already developed skills and strategies to decode and make sense of a variety of symbol systems, including print. Through this interaction, young children also appear to be developing motivations for reading and confidence in handling text as well as forming aspects of personal literary identity. However, The Oakfield Study data strongly suggests that many children may be at risk of losing these valuable strategies in order to comply with 'schooled' constructions of reading.

This has many implications for the early years educator. Firstly, it appears that part of the role of the Foundation Stage educator is to help children to value and build upon the strategies they develop at home to make sense of texts in general. This means that the schooling system needs to not only widen constructions of reading to include the reading of popular culture and media texts, but actively encourage children to value the strategies they are using to read such texts. Moreover, if young children are to value these strategies, then parents and carers must also be involved in the process and encouraged to recognise that reading is now a multimodal skill. From this position, early years educators can help children to build on these understandings and find new ways to read texts that embrace, rather than replace, their existing strategies.

This chapter has also suggested it is vital that young children are offered opportunities to engage with print in contexts that are meaningful. This includes the provision of opportunities for young children to interact with multimedia, such as computer texts, and for this engagement to be celebrated in the classroom. However, there is also evidence to suggest that Foundation Stage classrooms should reflect the individual lives and experiences of the children. This is perhaps especially important for Reception classes, where children may be exposed to more formalised constructions of reading. Issues raised in this chapter strongly suggest that there is an urgent need for teachers to find ways in which to embed print-literacy discourses within a wider discourse on reading that allows young children to develop confidence in themselves as readers of text, rather than readers (or indeed non-readers) of books alone.

Finally, this chapter provides evidence to suggest that the facilitative role of play needs to become more central within the early years curriculum. Given that learning to read appears to be something of a 'holistic' skill, it seems vital that young children are given substantial opportunities to engage with a wide variety of texts, which include symbolic representations, within the course of their daily play in school. Again this may have particular salience for the Reception classroom, and beyond. As children move into Reception and then Key Stage 1, play is often seen as a reward once the serious business of 'work' has been completed. However, findings raised in this chapter very much indicate that play-centred activity may serve a vital role in helping children to become experienced, confident and competent readers of text.

This very much supports the call for a change in the curriculum to allow teachers and children more space to build upon the ways in which texts are used in the home and in the wider community. Specific recommendations for practice are discussed in more detail towards the end of this book but it does appear that a general goal for early years education would be to find ways in which to allow aspects of children's home discourse to penetrate school boundaries. However, this is not a straightforward issue. On the basis of data discussed so far in this book, the next chapter looks specifically at the ways in which children are influenced by home and school constructions of reading, and examines what happens when the two discourses meet during the early years of schooling.

Key questions 🔑

- On the basis of issues raised in this chapter, how do you think computers should be used in Nursery and Reception classrooms?
- Apart from print, what other symbol systems do children use to make sense of texts?
- What can teachers do to encourage young children to value the strategies they bring into school to make sense of texts?
- How specifically can teachers embed aspects of print literacy within a wider discourse on reading?
- How can play be used in early years settings to encourage young children to experience and become confident in handling texts?

6

What reading means at home and at school

Chapter Overview

This book has so far described a number of factors that influence the ways in which young children form their own definitions of reading and perceptions of themselves as readers within the context of these definitions. While it appears that children draw upon their experiences of using a whole variety of texts, including books, digital technology and popular culture, this book has also shown that the settings within which children learn play a crucial role in influencing children's perceptions of reading. With this in mind, this chapter now examines the concept of home and school reading practices, and the ways in which continuities and discontinuities between these practices can influence children's perceptions of themselves as readers.

Of course, it has been widely documented that the home setting makes an especially important contribution to the ways in which children develop language and literacy skills (Tizard and Hughes, 1984; Cairney, 2003). It is clearly the case that children are indeed influenced by their families (Minns, 1997), culture (Brooker, 2002) and community structures (Heath, 1983) when it comes to the learning of literacy and language. As a result, much research has sought to understand 'family literacy' practices (Hannon and James, 1990; Saint-Laurent and Giasson, 2005), particularly in the attempt to integrate home and school experiences more effectively for children. However, by shifting the emphasis to the children's own perceptions, this book indicates that there is much to be gained from understanding what happens when the domains of home and school are brought into 'conversation' (Moje et al., 2004) during children's early years in school. As raised in the first chapter of this book, previous research has suggested that while transition into school may be comfortable for some children, certain issues such as culture (Brooker, 2002) and social class (Tudge et al., 2003) may serve to disadvantage others in that some young children may find that they must learn new rules or 'codes' (Bernstein, 1971) in order to function successfully in the school environment. As this book has highlighted, the same principle also appears to apply to the ways in which young children develop understandings about what reading is and what it means to be a reader. This indicates that many young children may be struggling to reconcile their own constructions of reading with the discourse operating in school and come to believe that they must comply with the codes of the classroom in order to be seen as a reader.

Since the mid-1990s, researchers operating within a variety of different disciplines have drawn upon a theory known as 'third space theory' (Bhabha, 1994) to help explore this notion of 'conversation' between two or more different discourses, particularly in relation to literacy practice. For example, Wilson (2000) used third space theory to investigate aspects of prisoners' literacies which were created in between the discourses of 'inside' and 'outside' prison. As a consequence, third space theory has been of particular interest to those seeking to develop continuity between home and school literacies. For example, Cook (2005: 87) attempted to bring 'home-type contexts and pedagogies' into classrooms through the creation of an established role-play area. The purpose of this area was to promote the production of 'unschooled texts', such as those used every day within family settings, but within the school setting. Yet Cook argued that the aim of this intervention was not just to bring home-type literacy discourse into school, but to explicate the connection between 'schooled' and 'unschooled' texts.

The purpose of this chapter is to use this concept of third space theory to critically reflect on the ways in which young children's perceptions of reading are influenced by their transition into the school setting (see Figure 6.1). As Marsh (2008) points out, while it is important to recognise that third space theory does have limitations, in that 'the worlds of educational institutions and homes/communities cannot be seen as two entirely separate domains', it does remain a 'useful metaphor when considering what happens when the different discourses embedded within childhood meet'. Having already described a variety of factors that influence the ways in which young children perceive reading, this

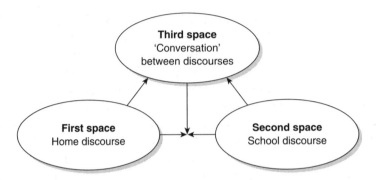

Figure 6.1   Application of 'third space theory'

chapter now uses the metaphor of 'third space' to examine the roles of home and school in shaping the ways in which young children develop beliefs about themselves as readers. The first part of this chapter draws on data gathered from the Nursery cohort within The Oakfield Study, as these children had less experience within the school system in comparison with the Reception cohort and therefore offered a greater opportunity to explore the influences of the school discourse.

Developing perceptions of reading during the Nursery year

Chapters 2 and 3 described the ways in which the Nursery children in The Oakfield Study developed perceptions of reading. Although these young children were clearly drawing from various aspects of their home literacy practices, the project data suggested that the school discourse was highly influential in the creation of these perceptions, even from the time of entry into the Nursery classroom. In particular, the extent to which print literacy featured within a definition of reading seemed to cause particular contention for these children when the discourses of home and school were brought into conversation during the Nursery year.

As reported, both Caitlyn and Kelly spoke positively about reading during their Nursery interviews, yet both girls also described it as a 'hard' thing to do, emphasising the need to decode print in texts. Neither girl identi-fied herself as being a reader because they both believed that they did not have the skills needed to decode words in books. Yet the project data highlighted that Caitlyn in particular had a great passion for books as well as an extraordinary ability to create narratives based upon pictures. However, even though Caitlyn could access much meaning from the pictures and could create sophisticated narratives based upon this, she clearly believed that reading was about decoding the print, reporting that she needed to 'see if they [words] sound' and 'if they're the right letters'.

This suggested that even in Nursery, Caitlyn was very aware that the school system emphasises a need to decode print in texts, despite the fact that both Caitlyn's mother and teacher reported that they believed that Caitlyn was either unaware of print or not especially interested in it. Yet Caitlyn's Nursery profile suggested that not only was Caitlyn aware of the role of print in texts, but she was also quite concerned about learning to decode it. As stated, many of her comments referred to reading as being 'word' based, which she regarded as 'hard' and which required a great deal of 'practice' to decode.

Like Caitlyn, Kelly also seemed aware of an impending expectation that she will soon have to learn to decode printed text in order to comply with the school's definition of 'reading'. In Nursery she too reported that learning to read is 'hard', explaining that this was because she 'can't read'. Yet in contrast to Caitlyn, rather than this being a concern it appeared to be something that she was looking forward to learning to do. What is more, Kelly's profile also suggested that she believed that she would learn to read once she was in Reception the following year. For example, she consistently reported that she would become a reader once she 'is five'.

As well as appearing more positive about the process of learning to decode printed text, Kelly's Nursery profile revealed that she did also have an interest in one particular aspect of letter knowledge: the letters in her name. It has been well documented that the letters in a child's name are 'tremendously important' (Scharer and Zutell, 2003: 274) for many children learning to read and write as it is often these letters that 'anchor the child's understanding that a specific written form consistently represents a particular meaning; a concept critical to future development' (2003: 275). As Scharer and Zutell go on to explain, the letters in a child's name often account for a substantial amount of the random letter writing done by 4- and 5-year-old children (Bloodgood, 1999). In turn, as children become more familiar with these letters, they begin to hypothesise about the ways in which these letters link to speech sounds and oral words. During the first home visit, Kelly was observed writing her name repeatedly on scraps of paper and twice reported that she 'can do' her name on the computer, when interviewed in school. As highlighted earlier, Kelly's mother also reported that Kelly will often point out certain letters from her name within the environment and enjoys finding the letters of her name when eating alphabet-shaped potato chips.

It could therefore be argued that at this stage, Kelly had created a comfortable third space in between the discourses of home and school. Although she recognised that she cannot yet 'do' the kind of reading that she believed was expected of a Reception-aged child, she seemed confident that this was attainable and believed that she would be reading (as defined by the school system) the following year. What is more, Kelly's interest in the letters in her name also helped to provide continuity between the discourses of home and school. While this interest embraced the school's construction of reading as being print dependent, Kelly also displayed a certain ownership of these phonetic interests, evident in her quest to spot 'her letters' in the environment with her parents, to write her name at home and at school, and in her enthusiasm to find 'her [potato] letters' in the home.

Similarly, Shaun appeared to have created a third space in between home and school that was anchored within his own interest in letters and phonics. While he seemed to understand that letters and phonics were valued within a school context, he retained a genuine personal interest in them. In other words, his Nursery profile suggested that he knew what would be expected of him in Reception in terms of learning to decode printed text, but as this matched his own interests it did not cause him concern.

This contrasts sharply with Caitlyn's Nursery profile, which portrayed a space in between home and school that was far less comfortable and fraught with contradiction. Despite the fact that Caitlyn was clearly passionate about books, this did not provide continuity for her between the discourses of home and school. On the contrary, Caitlyn was already reporting that she did not value her own picture-reading skills, even in Nursery, thus promoting a discontinuity between her own constructions of reading and her perceptions of what was expected from the school system. The third space in between home and school discourses on reading therefore provided contentious territory for Caitlyn, which risked the disruption of her own sophisticated constructions of reading.

Such issues seemed initially less relevant to Huda and Ibrihim, as neither child appeared to be defining 'reading' as the decoding of print during their Nursery year. Ibrihim in particular appeared very comfortable with his definition of reading as being largely dependent on picture cues. Although Ibrihim's mother reported that Ibrihim wanted to read books whenever his 6-year-old sister 'was doing it', which involved decoding print in reading scheme books, Ibrihim appeared confident that his strategies to make meaning from texts were authentic and reported that he was 'a reader'. Ibrihim's confidence in his own abilities to read meant that he appeared to have little difficulty in bridging the gap between home and school discourses on reading during his Nursery year. He valued his own picture-reading skills and regarded them as an authentic strategy in which to make meaning from texts and enjoyed using books in school and at home. This finding will come as no surprise to researchers such as Arizpe and Styles (2003: 224) who clearly demonstrated not only that children are 'extremely good at analysing the visual features of texts' but that young readers' responses to pictures can be deeply intellectual.

Like Ibrihim, Huda also appeared to believe that picture reading contributed towards a definition of 'reading' and that reading was really all about enjoying books. However, there was also evidence to suggest that Huda was aware that print reading does exist within definitions of reading. Yet during her Nursery year Huda appeared content to fit these conceptualisations of print reading within her broader constructions of reading. For example, she spoke regularly not only of reading with her mother at home, but of her mother reading a variety of texts such as newspapers. She seemed to accept that her own strategies to make meaning from texts were authentic and she did describe herself as 'a reader' although she appeared aware that there were some aspects of reading that her mother could do that she herself was unable to do as yet. This did not seem to be a concern for Huda though, who reported that 'mummies and daddies' and 'big girls' were all able to read, thus suggesting that she thought she would be able to decode print once she too was 'big' enough. It therefore appeared that the third space in between home and school discourses on reading was a comfortable area for Huda during her Nursery year. Firstly, she appeared happy to accept that her own strategies to make meaning from texts were authentic and of value. Secondly, although she seemed to believe that print reading was part of a larger definition of 'reading' she appeared to fit this within a wider conceptualisation created within her own home discourse.

Finally, David's story revealed that the Nursery can play a crucial role in helping children to develop a comfortable space in between home and school cultures. David's Nursery profile told the story of a young boy who had grown up in an environment dominated by superhero play. It has been well documented that aspects of popular culture can provide opportunities and motivation for children to engage with text and enter into dialogues about narrative and text (Arthur, 2005). However, superhero play has been seen to provide particularly fertile territory for young children to develop literary identities (Marsh, 1999; 2000; Dyson, 1997). Not only was this certainly seen to be the case for David, but superhero play also seemed to provide continuity for David between the domains of home and school. While David was observed watching superhero videos and playing with superhero figures independently at home, the Nursery school also provided artefacts and dressing up clothes which David used almost daily to create superhero role-play scenarios with his friends.

When interviewed during the Nursery year it therefore came as no surprise that David spoke of school in terms of play, providing rich descriptions of the superhero play he engaged in with his friends. He did not seem to regard school in terms of teaching or learning, and neither did he appear to be aware of an active or impending process to teach him to read. Yet his profile revealed that he was evidently learning to read iconic and printed images through the media of popular culture, television and play. As described in Chapter 2, this was strikingly apparent during the Popular Culture activity in Phase 1, where David demonstrated a remarkable ability to match print and iconic popular culture cards together. The result was surprising as neither David's mother nor teacher believed that David had any awareness or interest in letter recognition. Yet findings from the study revealed that David was indeed learning to recognise printed images.

However, this learning appeared to be taking place through David's utilisation of media such as play and television texts, without any specific adult intervention. Therefore David appeared to have created a space for himself situated in play and popular culture that offered continuity between home and school cultures. What is more, it appeared that the structure of David's Nursery school encouraged him to develop his understandings of print by allowing him the space to make these connections for himself. Yet, as highlighted in Chapter 3, once David moved into Reception these interactions with print seemed to degenerate. This suggests that entry into Reception triggered a significant change in the ways in which David was integrating home and school constructions of reading, which in turn had a major impact on how he began to see himself in terms of ability in reading. Moreover, David was not the only child from the Nursery cohort to experience such disruption on entry into Reception. By maintaining a focus on the 'conversation' between home and school discourses on reading, the next section looks at how the move into Reception influenced the ways in which these six Nursery children saw themselves as readers.

Moving into Reception – changes in the third space

As already demonstrated, all of the children in The Oakfield Study came to believe that the school system defined reading as the ability to decode words in books (and in reading scheme books in particular). Yet, recognising that many of the Nursery children entered the schooling system with broad definitions of reading, this raises questions about the ways in which continuities and discontinuities between the discourses of home and school influence young children's perceptions and beliefs about reading as they move through their Reception year in school.

As Shaun progressed through Reception, home and schooled discourses on reading appeared to merge comfortably. Although he did not appear to include print decoding within his own definitions of reading when he was in Nursery, he did not seem concerned by this change in construction when he moved into Reception. Firstly, Shaun seemed genuinely interested in letters, words and phonics which meant that he appeared to enjoy learning to decode printed text in Reception. Yet he also continued to report that he valued a variety of other strategies to make meaning from texts. This suggested that although Shaun did become proficient in decoding print, he continued to use a variety of strategies to make meaning from texts, including the use of picture and contextual cues. Secondly, the emphasis on learning to decode print in reading scheme texts also appeared to be viewed positively by Shaun. For example, Shaun's family reported that they valued the time that they spent with Shaun and his sister each evening when they looked at the reading scheme books together. This supports Cairney's assertion that 'shared reading plays a key role in family literacy practices' (2003: 87). In this respect the reading scheme books themselves became integrated into Shaun's family culture. In fact it is also worth noting that during the Smiley Face activity Shaun rated *Reading your school book to an adult* as a 'happy face' in his home context, but only rated it as a 'middle face' in school. This again suggests that Shaun enjoyed reading his reading scheme books to his family in the evenings, thus further promoting a comfortable continuity between home and school discourses on reading.

Moreover, as discussed in Chapter 5, Shaun appeared to have acquired a particular fluency in using aspects of digital technology which also seemed to provide something of a 'middle ground' in between the discourses of home and school. Although access to computer technology was minimal within Shaun's home environment, he was seen to have developed sophisticated competencies in using computers within the

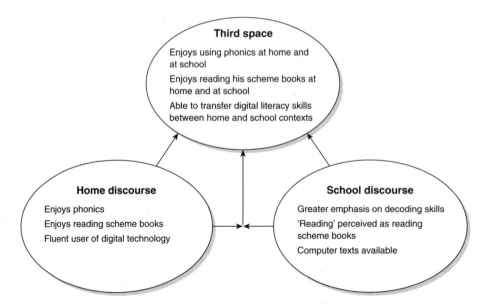

Figure 6.2   Shaun: third space in between discourses of home and school

school environment. Recognising that Shaun did in fact use a variety of other digital multimedia at home, it appeared that he had developed something of a 'digital literacy' (Glister, 1997) that allowed him to use and enjoy new and unfamiliar digital technologies with competence. Throughout all three phases of the study, Shaun demonstrated that he could indeed transfer these skills from one medium or setting to another, thus suggesting that digital technologies in themselves had allowed Shaun to comfortably cross the boundaries of home and school. Subsequently, the transference of digital skill together with Shaun's interest in letters and phonics appeared to have created a comfortable third space in between the discourses of home and school, as illustrated in Figure 6.2.

Ibrihim also appeared comfortable with the move into Reception although it was clear that his own constructions of reading changed during this period. While his Nursery profile suggested that he largely did not include print literacy within his definition of reading, by the second phase of the study he was reporting that reading was very much about decoding print. It was clear that Ibrihim believed that it was not easy to develop decoding skills, but this did not mean that he had developed a negative attitude towards reading. Firstly, like Shaun it appeared that Ibrihim quite enjoyed the process of learning to decode print. What is more, even though Ibrihim reported that it was 'hard' to learn to decode print, he embraced it as something of a challenge and appeared to derive particular satisfaction from seeing himself move through the stages of his reading scheme. Indeed, Ofsted (2004) noted that in many schools children did see reading schemes as something to be worked through until they were able to attain the status of being a 'free reader' (2004: 11). One can see how some children may enjoy this process if they are regularly being moved up from one level to another. However, as discussed in Chapter 4, unless a child is moving swiftly through the stages of the scheme this can easily lead to discouragement.

It therefore appeared that Ibrihim accommodated the new 'schooled' discourse on reading partly by accepting the challenge that it offered. However, the project data also provides a warning. Although Ibrihim appeared happy to accept this challenge, his Phase 2 profile suggested that he, like others in the sample, was already beginning to believe that he was unable to read books outside of his reading scheme. This therefore warns that although Ibrihim seemed to enjoy the new challenge offered by the schooled discourse on reading, this discourse was already threatening to disrupt rather than build upon Ibrihim's own 'home' constructions of reading, where he was learning to make sense of and enjoy different types of reading media.

Similarly, Huda was also faced with a new construction of reading on entry into Reception. While her Nursery profile suggested that although she did seem to believe that print reading contributed towards a definition of 'reading', Huda appeared happy to fit this within a broader construction. Yet by the second phase of the study, Huda's definition of 'reading' appeared to have narrowed to the extent of believing that reading was largely the decoding of print in reading scheme books. Once again, this change was seen to intrude upon existing constructions of reading. Like Ibrihim, Huda also reported that she could not read books outside of her reading scheme in Phase 2, yet she did not embrace the reading scheme as a challenge. On the contrary, the second-phase data suggested that Huda's confidence in reading very much diminished on entry into Reception, with classroom observations suggesting that Huda lost much of the interest and enjoyment of books that was evident in Nursery.

These cases indicate that while there is indeed value in understanding how the discourses of home and school influence young children's perceptions of reading, it is also important to recognise how the 'meeting' of these two discourses can have an impact on young children. As Bearne and Marsh (2007) highlight, when discourses such as those of the home and the school are brought together, the space in between can be 'uncomfortable'. Huda's profile suggested that this was certainly true in her case. However, this issue was further magnified in the cases of David, Caitlyn and Kelly.

David's profile told the story of a young boy who was learning to make sense of print during his Nursery year through the context of play, popular culture and television texts. Yet as David moved into Reception his engagement with print seemed to disappear. The Reception curriculum presented a discourse on reading that not only had little meaning for David but actually appeared to impede his own developing constructions of reading. What is more, there is evidence throughout David's profile to suggest that even though the school discourse on reading had little meaning for him, he was still trying to reconcile this with his own 'home' constructions. For example, David became clearly excited when shown a flashcard with the word 'Dad' during a guided reading session, stating that he recognised that the first two letters were in his own name. Given that it has already been noted that the letters in a child's name are extremely important for children learning to read and write (Scharer and Zutell, 2003), it is clear that this was one way in which printed letters were meaningful for David. What is more, David's teacher stated in the final stage of the study, that instead of reading the print in his books, David would rather 'talk about things that the book reminds him of' or 'talk about Spiderman in relation to that book'. This again illustrates that for David, literacy needed to be anchored within a meaningful context that connected strongly with his own interests. Given that David had a passionate interest in superhero play, it is particularly fascinating to observe that he was drawing from this aspect of popular culture in order to establish his own links with schooled reading (for more research on the role of superhero play see Marsh, 1999; 2000; Dyson, 1997).

This resonates strongly with the work of Pahl (2002) who closely studied three young boys' text production in the home. Having established that these boys regularly produced what she called 'ephemeral' texts, which were often produced from the 'momentary' artefacts of everyday life (such as bits of food, tissues and so on), she argued that much could be learned about these boys' literate understandings. However, David's story revealed that he was not only developing a sound literary identity within the constructions of his home discourse, but was grappling to find a way in which to connect this to the expectations of school. Yet the project data revealed that in doing so, he was not only at risk of losing connections with his own understandings of reading and print literacy, but also losing confidence in himself as a reader.

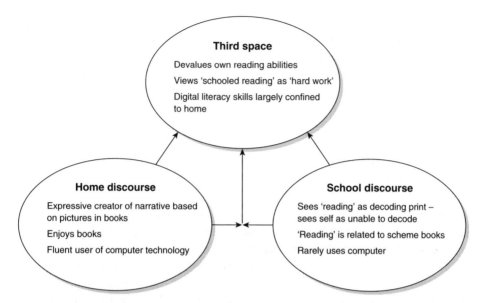

Figure 6.3 Caitlyn: third space in between discourses of home and school

Similar issues were identified in the cases of Caitlyn and Kelly. Unlike David, both girls appeared to have recognised that the school discourse on reading is connected to print decoding, even when they were in Nursery. Subsequently, the move into Reception did not reveal a *new* construction of reading as such, but did further narrow their perception of reading in that they came to believe that they had to learn to decode print in their reading scheme books in order to be seen to be 'a reader'. As was particularly evident in the case of Caitlyn, this perception was met with anxiety as she believed that she was unable to decode printed text. Yet Caitlyn was also seen to have a great passion for books, but the strategies that she used herself to make meaning from texts did not fit with her perceptions of a schooled discourse in reading. Subsequently, the gap between 'schooled' reading and 'home' reading appeared to widen throughout the year of data collection, as illustrated in Figure 6.3.

This chapter has used the lens of third space theory (Moje et al., 2004) to take a fresh look at the ways in which the discourses of home and school can influence how young children develop perceptions of themselves as readers. In particular this chapter has shown that children's valuable 'home' constructions of reading can become dissolved when the discourses of home and school are brought into 'conversation' during the early years of schooling. However, findings from The Oakfield

Study further suggest that parents as well as children can find themselves struggling to reconcile the opposing discourses of home and school. The next section demonstrates how some of the mothers in The Oakfield Study also experienced contention in the third space between the discourses of home and school, as their children moved through their first years at school.

Parents: confidence and contention in the third space

Having established that Caitlyn experienced considerable discomfort in her attempt to reconcile the discourses of home and school, it is interesting to note that this unease was also acknowledged by Caitlyn's mother, who was herself a teacher in Caitlyn's school. Firstly, it was apparent that Caitlyn's mother was aware that a separation did indeed exist between Caitlyn's home and school reading. She reported that although Caitlyn still clearly enjoyed reading books in the home, either alone or with other members of the family, Caitlyn was 'quite reluctant' to read her reading scheme book to her. This seemed to surprise Caitlyn's mother who reported that she would have expected Caitlyn to want to read these books to her, given her passion for books in general.

However, Caitlyn's mother did acknowledge that there were issues surrounding the strategies Caitlyn used to read books at home and at school, and that Caitlyn's 'home' reading did not fit within the school discourse. She reported that even though Caitlyn now 'has a bank of key words' and is able to decode aspects of printed text, she still elects to 'read books [from] her head' and 'tell the story herself' when reading books at home, rather than decode the words. When asked how she feels about Caitlyn's reading, her mother reported that when she is wearing her 'teacher's hat', she still feels slightly concerned about Caitlyn's 'level' in reading, which is defined by an ability to employ decoding strategies. However, she also appeared to continue to place great value on Caitlyn's 'storytelling' skills which she described as 'incredible'. It therefore appears that to some extent Caitlyn's own constructions of reading have had an influence upon Caitlyn's mother's perceptions of the ways in which reading is taught in schools. As a class teacher and literacy co-ordinator herself, Caitlyn's mother reported that although she is very happy with the way reading is generally taught, she would prefer to see a broadening of the curriculum. She stated:

I don't know how much time they give to what Caitlyn's good at – the storytelling skills – which I think translate into writing ... setting up a scene with the Playmobile and allowing the children to tell a story and record it or tell it to the rest of the class – which I think is a really important reading skill as well. I don't know how much of that goes on – but I'd like to see more of it I feel.

As well as introducing storytelling skills into the curriculum, Caitlyn's mother also reported that she would like to see the children in school being allowed to take home a wider selection of books, extending beyond those in the reading scheme. Moreover, she also spoke of her desire to see a 'broadening' of the way in which reading is taught, to include teaching children the skills to 'navigate round the page' on the internet and to scan screen or paper texts for 'important information'. This suggests that the disparity between home and schooled discourses on reading is not just a problem for Caitlyn but for her mother also. While on the one hand she values Caitlyn's home constructions of reading and has articulated a desire to see such constructions valued in school, on the other hand she cannot suppress her concern that Caitlyn has not reached the expected 'level' in reading as defined by her ability to decode print in her reading scheme. It is particularly noteworthy that Caitlyn's mother herself places this concern within the realms of the school discourse, by referring to the concept of wearing her 'teacher's hat'.

Yet Caitlyn's mother was not the only parent to recognise this dichotomy between home and schooled reading. Kelly's mother also reported that although Kelly enjoys reading her school book in the evening, she 'enjoys telling the story even more'. As reported, Kelly's mother also observed a difference in the way in which Kelly reads her schoolbook and her own 'longer' books in the home. She reported that when Kelly is looking at her own books in the home she is 'not reading word for word, but she'll look at the pictures' and will be 'putting a lot of expression in'. Yet Kelly's mother stated that when Kelly is 'reading her schoolbook, her reading is quite monotonous, but when she's reading from her head she uses quite a lot of expression'.

While it has certainly been reported that many parents feel insecure about their own abilities to support their children's schooling, particularly in terms of using the 'correct' techniques in the home to match the expectations of school (Hannon and James, 1990; Oritz and Stile, 1996), it is interesting to note that both of these mothers are recognising that there are elements of school literacy practice (also referred to as 'school-centric literacies' by Knobel and Lankshear, 2003) that are actually obstructive. This again suggests that both of these mothers are themselves struggling to reconcile the expectations of the school discourse with the reading skills their children have developed in the home.

Similarly Malcolm's mother (Reception cohort) reported that she was worried that Malcolm may struggle with aspects of the literacy curriculum because he was one of the youngest children in the class. She stated that her 'biggest concern is just that he (Malcolm) doesn't fall too behind or sort of becomes frustrated' because he cannot keep up with the others in his class. Bearing in mind that although Malcolm's Year 1 teacher reported that he 'tries really hard' with his reading and has 'got the right attitude that he needs to do it', she also reported that he finds it 'very hard' to decode printed text and as a result is in the lowest reading group in the class. This does seem to provide a degree of discomfort for Malcolm's mother who stressed that Malcolm was 'so tired by the end of the day, coming home from school' that reading his scheme book became 'hard work' for him. However, she further reported that she felt Malcolm was doing 'fantastically well' with his letter recognition and general progress in reading. This again suggests that although Malcolm's mother seems very happy with Malcolm's current ability in reading, given that he is so young in the year, she is worried that he may become frustrated by the fact that he is not yet able to produce the kind of reading that is expected by the schooling system.

While it is clear that the comments provided by these three mothers suggest that they were indeed all concerned that aspects of the school discourse on reading could have a negative effect on their children's engagement with reading, it is probably fair to say that each mother had sufficient 'cultural capital' (Brooker, 2002) of her own to be able to reflect somewhat critically on the discourses of home and school, and as a result could modify aspects of 'home-reading' activity herself to help build bridges between the two settings. For example, Malcolm's mother reported that if Malcolm was ever too tired to read his school book in the evening, she would read the book to him instead and would 'put the wrong word in and see if it catches him out', which he would find amusing. This was clearly a skilful way in which to encourage Malcolm to focus on the printed text, without making him actually read the whole book himself. In this respect Malcolm's mother had found a way in which to respond to the requirements of the school curriculum within the context of their own home discourse.

Yet, given that it has been documented that many parents worry that they are not using the 'correct' methods of instruction with their children

(Oritz and Stile, 1996) as defined by the school discourse, it is easy to see that some parents may not have the confidence or the skills to construct such bridge-building activity into their home discourse. Certainly issues of confidence were highly evident in Annie's (Reception cohort) profile, both in relation to herself and her mother as discussed below.

Like Malcolm, Annie also appeared to be trying very hard to conform to a schooled discourse on reading. As highlighted in Chapter 4, Annie's lack of confidence in herself as a reader meant that she displayed a great sense of dependence on her reading scheme and was very concerned about tackling not only those texts that existed outside of the reading scheme, but even reading scheme texts that were not of her assigned colour band. Yet for Annie, issues of confidence were especially salient as her mother also reported a great lack of confidence in reading. Annie's mother reported that she herself had felt highly intimidated by reading when she was at school and was particularly unhappy about being made to read out loud when she was at secondary school. She stated:

> I was really nervous – really scared. I would always sit at the back of the class hoping that I wouldn't be picked [to read] ... and I'd sort of skip ahead in the book and try and read bits so that I could read it out to myself so that I would know I'd be all right reading out to the whole class. I would just get so scared. It was horrible.

Annie's mother further reported that as a result of such insecurities, little reading takes place in her home today. Having stated that she herself has to 'read out loud' in order for texts 'to make sense', she reported that she feels too embarrassed to read in front of other people and so 'just doesn't bother reading'. As book reading is evidently a highly contentious issue for Annie's mother, it was not surprising that she also reported that the family have very few books in the house. As Annie has evidently been witness to her mother's own insecurities about reading, presented largely as an intimidating activity, it is not difficult to understand why Annie may herself have a particular struggle to develop confidence in reading. Annie's case illustrates how the school discourses on reading can affect young children even before they enter the formal education system themselves. In Annie's case, the home discourse on reading will very likely have been influenced by her mother's negative experiences with schooled reading. What is more, given that both Annie and her mother appeared to have little confidence in their own reading abilities, it is easy to see why Annie may have developed such a dependence on the school discourse and the reading scheme in particular.

Yet as has been clearly documented in this study, there is evidence to suggest that such dependencies can be dangerous. As observed, progress through a reading scheme was seen to actively discourage many of the children in The Oakfield Study from attempting to read texts existing outside of the scheme. Given that the reading scheme was also perceived as defining one's status as a reader, the scheme often endorsed children's negative perceptions of themselves as readers. It therefore seems the case that Annie would have benefited from being given opportunities to broaden her perceptions of reading and engage with a variety of strategies to make meaning from paper- and screen-based texts, rather than being further constrained by the narrow definitions of a schooled discourse in reading.

☐ Summary

Using The Oakfield Study as a sustained source of reference, this book has shown how young children may enter the school system with sophisticated constructions of reading. These constructions offer real value to the children in terms of building confidence in themselves as readers as well as allowing them to develop strategies to make meaning from texts. These strategies include the handling of multimodal cues, interactions with print, picture reading, symbolic understandings, book knowledge and the use of digital literacies. Many of these strategies were seen to work together providing a holistic definition of reading, which often originated within a home discourse on reading.

Using aspects of third space theory to explore this issue further, this chapter has reported on the ways in which children can create spaces in between home and schooled discourses when they first enter the formal education system. Yet it is clear that these valuable constructions of reading can be threatened by the dominant discourse of school when the two discourses of home and school are brought into 'conversation'. What is more, this chapter has revealed that such discontinuities between the domains of home and school can cause disruption for parents as well as children, as they struggle to reconcile an established 'home' discourse with what is often perceived to be the 'correct' discourse of the school.

Building upon this, the following chapters now focus squarely on the implications of these issues. By focusing attention on the role of the early years practitioner, Chapters 7 and 8 explore how the issues raised in this book can inform early years practice and encourage young children to develop motivation and confidence in themselves as readers.

Key questions 🔑

- What strategies can early years practitioners employ in order to ensure that continuity exists between the reading discourses of home and school?
- In what ways can children's names be used as a stimulus for letter recognition in the classroom?
- How can early years practitioners build upon children's meaningful engagement with texts in the home?
- How can early years practitioners demonstrate that they value children's home reading experiences?
- What can teachers do to promote confidence in parents with regard to their children's progress in reading?

7

From research to practice

Chapter Overview

How should we be teaching children to learn to read in schools today? Sadly, this book cannot, and indeed does not attempt to, provide a formula or recipe for how to teach reading. In fact the findings from The Oakfield Study strongly suggest that formulaic approaches to the teaching of reading are not in the best interests of many young children. However, this does not mean that the teaching of reading should be unstructured. On the contrary, this book has highlighted that learning to read is a complex yet unique process for each individual child, and is embedded within their own dynamic socio-cultural constructions of the world around them. What is more, this world in which these children live is changing; children's experience of text no longer relates to paper-based contexts alone, but includes the reading of a whole range of digital and screen media (Marsh et al., 2005; Carrington, 2005). As a consequence, this study suggests that practitioners need to recognise such shifts and find ways in which to support individual children in their journey towards reading literacy. This is not to suggest, of course, that practitioners need to plan individual programmes of study to meet the separate needs of each child in their class. Rather, this book is urging teachers of young children to critically reflect on the ways in which practice can be modified in order to address the issues that have been raised in this book. While serious concerns about current policy on the teaching of reading in early years have indeed been raised, the study at the centre of this book also suggests that implications for practice can include quite a subtle shift, for example, in how we think about reading, talk about it with children and parents, and in the terminology we use during reading instruction. The purpose of this chapter is therefore to examine the implications of the research described in this book for teachers and practitioners working in early years settings. In particular, this chapter aims to encourage reflection on aspects of practice that may influence children's confidence and motivation for reading from their earliest years in school.

Perceptions of reading

One of the most striking findings from The Oakfield Study related to the ways in which the children formed their own definitions of reading. As demonstrated in Chapters 2 and 3, the Nursery cohort entered the schooling system with broad definitions of reading that included a wide variety of strategies to make sense of texts. However, the study further revealed that all twelve children were highly influenced by the school discourse on reading from Reception onwards, which seemed to promote the message that reading was really all about decoding print, especially within the context of reading scheme texts.

Of course it is important to point out that it is highly unusual for teachers to focus solely on phonics instruction in their day-to-day teaching and to discourage children from recognising that strategies such as picture reading can contribute towards their acquisition of meaning. On the contrary, most teachers acknowledge that such strategies are valuable and do include them as a matter of course within their reading instruction activity. However, it must be recognised that given the current climate where synthetic phonics is taking an increasingly central role in the teaching of reading, it is likely that the curriculum, together with its assessment, will have an influence on how children define what reading is as well as develop perceptions of themselves as readers.

Findings from The Oakfield Study strongly suggested that for many children, the perception that reading *is* largely the decoding of print led to poor self-perceptions and a lack of confidence in reading from Reception onwards. In some cases even Nursery-aged children reported that they were unable to read because they could not decode print. This suggests that teachers should not only be continuing to encourage children to include strategies such as picture reading and the use of contextual clues in their reading, but need to be alert to the fact that children's perceptions of reading are likely to be influenced by a wide variety of socio-political and socio-cultural factors. In particular, teachers should try to raise their own awareness of the subtle, more nuanced ways in which 'messages' about what reading is, and what it means to be 'good at reading', get transmitted to young children. For example, if the 'reading corner' in a classroom just has books on display, then this will indicate that 'school says' that reading is a book-related activity. However, if the reading corner contains a variety of multimodal texts (including comics, magazines, screen texts and so on) then this will send a different message to the children about what reading is.

It is also useful to consider the ways in which messages about 'what counts' as reading emerge from within school settings. In particular, ways in which children receive clues about 'what counts' as reading may be embedded in the language teachers use in their day-to-day classroom activity. The following questions and examples illustrate how teachers can broaden definitions of reading and encourage children to view reading as a multimodal skill.

- *When children read numerical symbols, are they told that they have read well? Or is the reading of numerical symbols confined to a 'maths' discourse which is deemed to have little to do with reading?* By acknowledging that the decoding of symbols, such as numbers, car badge signs, road signs, logos and so on, is part of reading in the same way as the decoding of letters is part of reading, children can be encouraged to value the range of symbolic systems that are in existence in texts today as well as the strategies they develop to decode these symbols.

- *What language do you use when you refer to pictures and print in text?* If teachers talk about 'looking' at pictures and 'reading' print, then this will immediately devalue the role of picture reading in the deconstruction of text. By asking children whether they would prefer to read the pictures or the print first for example, or perhaps telling children that they have read the pictures well, teachers will be demonstrating that they value the decoding of pictures as well as the decoding of print.

- *Are children encouraged to think about the reader when drawing their own pictures within texts?* Children in early years settings are regularly invited to draw pictures to accompany printed text that they produce. However, very often these pictures are viewed as a secondary activity, only to be drawn once the real business of writing letters and words has been performed. Yet children can be invited to think about ways in which to develop their pictures in order to help the reader find further meaning from the words. This encourages children to not only value picture reading, but think critically about the ways in which words and pictures work together in the construction and deconstruction of text.

- *Do you ever invite children to come and read a screen text with you? What language do you tend to use in connection with the decoding of screen texts?* If you find that you only use the word 'reading' in reference to the decoding of print on the screen, then this could send the message that reading is only about 'the words' even when reading screen texts. When talking to children about reading screen texts, ensure that you make reference to the whole text (pictures, symbols, hyperlinks, icons) and discuss the fact that the print can be used alongside these other symbols and images in order to help the reader understand what is on the screen.

These are just a few examples to illustrate some of the various ways in which teachers can begin to encourage young children to value a wide range of strategies to make sense of texts. It is important to point out that none of this is intended to devalue the role of print in text – indeed it is extremely important that young children are offered opportunities to understand how print works and recognise its role in meaning making. However, as The Oakfield Study highlighted, there is a danger that an overemphasis on decoding print, particularly during the Foundation Stage, can promote feelings of failure in young children from their earliest years in school. This cannot be overlooked, especially given that large-scale study into reading achievement and attitude towards reading indicates that children in the UK perform poorly in comparison with children from many other countries. The PIRLS (NFER, 2003) produced comparable data on the reading achievement of 10-year-old children within 35 countries. Solity and Vousden (2009: 474) draw our attention to the fact that the 2003 report (NFER, 2003) indicated that 'although children from England came third out of 35 countries on measures of reading accuracy, they scored poorly in terms of attitude towards reading [and] read less often for fun than pupils in comparable countries'. Following this, the 2006 PIRLS (Twist et al., 2007) reported that England had now dropped to fifteenth place in terms of reading accuracy and that attitudes towards reading were continuing to decline.

Given that we do indeed commence formal education in the UK far earlier than in other comparable countries, it does seem imperative that we pay urgent attention to the ways in which young children in the Foundation Stage and Key Stage 1 develop attitudes, confidence and motivation for reading. Bearing in mind the issues already raised, it is hugely important that we do not allow young children to see themselves as unsuccessful in reading during these early years. While it is of course very difficult to entirely remove issues of proficiency judgement from the classroom environment, this book suggests that rather than providing a discourse on reading that is defined by an ability to decode print, the Foundation Stage should be a period in which to encourage children to test out and experiment with a whole variety of strategies to make sense of texts that build upon those they have learned in their home environments. In order to do this, we must offer children copious opportunity to play. There is nothing new about this – early years practitioners have known for years that play is vital for young children's emotional, physical, social and intellectual development (Isaacs, 1930; Garvey, 1977; Donaldson, 1978; Moyles, 1989). However, given the prescriptive nature of the current curriculum, teachers may find themselves struggling to reconcile the demands of the curriculum with the need to provide play opportunities for their children. Moreover, there are also many different ways in which the concept of play can be both interpreted and implemented, so it is important that we are clear on how we intend to use play in the classroom. With this in mind, the following section reflects on some of the ways in which teachers can use play, and play-centred concepts, to encourage young children to develop strategies to make sense of texts and acquire motivations for reading.

Role of play

The Oakfield Study revealed that for many of the children studied, it was clear that they were not only learning to make sense of texts through their engagement with play-centred activity, but were developing specific understandings about aspects of textual analysis such as the role of print. This was perhaps especially evident in the case of David, who was seen to be making sense of print through the context of play, popular culture and television (see Chapter 2) during his Nursery year. Yet the formalisation of the curriculum during his Reception year appeared to actively prevent him from continuing to develop these understandings. This suggests that for children like David, it is imperative that opportunities to play remain central to classroom activity during Reception. Moreover, David's story further suggests that for some children, opportunities to engage in role play are especially important and can be a useful avenue in which to expose children to a wide variety of sign and symbol systems. While it has already been well documented that young children very often draw upon their interactions with superhero play when developing literary identity (Marsh, 1999, 2000;

Dyson, 1997), any form of role play can encourage children to position themselves within texts and therefore 'develop capacities necessary for reading' (Lysaker, 2006: 51).

However, in order to appreciate the ways in which role-play activity can support development in reading within an early years setting, it is necessary to return to the question of definition. If we regard reading as a narrow construction, largely limited to the decoding of print, then it is difficult to fully accept the value of such play in helping children to learn to read. However, this book has argued strongly that reading should be regarded as a broad, inclusive and holistic activity within early years settings. In other words, if we define reading as the capacity to, among other things, make sense of a range of sign and symbol systems, find meaning in texts, enter 'text worlds', enjoy texts and develop confidence in handling texts, then it becomes easier to see how engagement with role play can support such objectives.

Of course, in order for practitioners to really capitalise upon the opportunities play can offer within the early years setting, they do need to have an understanding of what is meaningful to the children in their class. If we look closely at the ways in which young children choose to structure their own play, we may find that we can learn much about what is meaningful to them. Moyles (1989: xi) points out that play therefore has a particular benefit within educational situations as it provides 'not only a real medium for learning but enables discerning and knowledgeable adults to learn about children and their needs'. This was illustrated beautifully in the work of Wohlwend (2009) who recently observed a young child making his own mobile phone from a piece of card within a classroom where few opportunities were offered to interact with the kinds of new media and technologies that were part of this child's everyday life. By observing this child at play, Wohlwend was able to acquire an understanding of this child's relationship with technology and thus gain knowledge about what was meaningful to him.

This example also shows that children are often very good at finding their own ways in which to make meaning from situations, by latching onto something that makes sense to them. However, if teachers are able to gain an awareness of what is important to the children in their class, and how they learn as individuals, then they can structure play-centred activities with more success. For example, although it cannot be assumed that all children entering the formal education system are immersed in particular aspects of popular culture, it is likely that some will be. By understanding which features of popular culture are meaningful to the children, teachers can then use this knowledge to structure role-play activity, introduce particular texts (including books, screen texts, posters, etc.), point out or create symbolic structures that are relevant to this aspect of popular culture (including print, logos, icons, etc.) or simply use this knowledge to initiate discussions or to help the children find meaning within classroom activity that may otherwise seem a little abstract to them. This is perhaps especially important during the Reception year, when it is expected that children will be exposed to more formalised methods of reading instruction. This is discussed in more detail later in this chapter.

So for purposes of clarity, the intention here is not to tell teachers and early years practitioners how to use play within the Foundation Stage. Rather, on the basis of findings from The Oakfield Study, this book is urging teachers and practitioners to challenge the view that reading is a narrow construction and promote it as an enjoyable, interactive activity that is firmly situated within a playful discourse. Moreover, it is a further intention that teachers acknowledge that reading education can be developed in accordance with the individual needs and interests of children in the class. While it is recognised that the Foundation Curriculum is target driven in nature, this book is urging teachers to ensure that the ways in which they personally think about reading, define it and promote it to young children are not constrained by the demands of the curriculum. This has major implications for the role of teachers within early years settings, particularly with regard to the relationship they develop with the children they are teaching.

The teacher–pupil relationship

There is no doubt that any teacher–pupil relationship is special. However, teachers and practitioners who work with young children are perhaps in a particularly interesting and challenging position. As children enter the formal education system, they are not only learning about the world around them, they are also learning what it means to be a learner – and in particular, what it means to be a learner in school. This places a huge responsibility on teachers within early years settings, as they are in the privileged position of not only teaching children, but teaching them how to learn.

This has particular implications for the ways in which the acquisition of knowledge is perceived by teachers. Hare (1992) argues that teachers have a responsibility to ensure that children understand that knowledge is tentative and that teachers' own answers are not always 'the best'. In his iconic publication, *Children's Thinking*, Bonnett (1994) asserts that this issue has a particular relevance for teachers and children working in early years settings. He argues that in order to encourage children to be effective learners, we must be willing to share a sense of 'wonderment' and 'astonishment' with them at what is being learned. In other words, it is being argued that teachers need to respond to young children in a manner that offers mutual interest in what is being learned, is non-evaluative and non-judgemental, and that children need to know that their responses are being taken seriously.

This is not to say that teachers should simply accept inaccurate comments from children. Indeed, as Hare (1992) argues, in order for teachers to teach, they must be an authority, though this is not the same as being 'in authority'. Therefore, respect for knowledge means that inaccurate responses should not go unchecked. However, if teachers enter into a relationship of mutual engagement with their children where education is viewed as an initiation into human life rather than a curriculum to be delivered, then they will be able to encourage children to develop their own relationships with learning in general.

This resonates strongly with the assertions raised in this chapter. It has so far been argued that as children enter the schooling system during the Foundation Stage, the main objective for teachers with regard to reading education should be to encourage young children to develop a variety of strategies to make sense of texts, develop confidence in handling a variety of different texts and acquire the motivation to read. By entering into a relationship of shared concern for knowledge, where teachers allow themselves to experience the 'wonder' of learning along with the children rather than positioning themselves as an authority on 'how to learn to read', teachers can provide meaningful opportunities for children to develop their own strategies to make sense of texts within a context that is free from proficiency grading. This does of course require discernment, energy and skill on the part of the teacher. Moreover, such an approach also requires that teachers have the confidence to immerse themselves in the learning experience with the children, and allow themselves to be led by the interests of the individual children with whom they are working.

In other words, much of what is being proposed here relates to a general ethos and a state of positioning, rather than offering structured suggestions for teaching. For this reason, there is little attempt being made here to offer practical suggestions for classroom activity, as the intention is that teachers will find their own ways in which to engage with reading activity and create meaningful encounters with the children in their class. However, there are some particular issues that teachers may like to consider. For example, how are questions used in the course of day-to-day interaction with the children? Is it the case that the questions asked to children in the classroom are always those that the teacher already knows the answers to? While teachers clearly need to ask such questions from time to time, this does little to promote the view that teachers are engaged with the learning process alongside the children. Perhaps teachers and practitioners could try and use 'questioning techniques' rather than questions (*I wonder what this says here?*) or ensure that the questions they do ask do not always have 'correct' or established answers (*What is the girl in this picture thinking? How would you feel if you were this boy in the story?*).

It is also important that children see that their teachers use and make reference to reading in relation to a variety of different contexts and that they use and value various strategies to make sense of texts. For example, teachers could introduce the children to characters in a Small World Play scenario and discuss the fact that these people are reading on computer screens, reading music, reading pictures and so on. Moreover, teachers could also ensure that children see that they are using various strategies themselves in their own reading that include, but are not limited to, the decoding of print. (*I think I know what is happening on this page because I can see a picture of a dog trying to climb up the tree.*) Much of what is being recommended here cannot be planned in a structured sense; rather this chapter is urging teachers to make the most of opportunities for learning as they arise within the classroom. By entering into games and role-play activity with young children, teachers and practitioners are likely to find that such opportunities arise freely and naturally enabling them to participate in the learning process along with the children.

So far this chapter has attempted to encourage teachers working in early years settings to find various ways in which to promote reading as a broad construct that draws upon multimodal skills and that relates to a variety of different modes and media. Moreover, it has also been further recommended that teachers actively engage with the learning experience alongside children and show that they too are involved in processes of meaning acquisition. However, it is recognised that this may be easier to achieve for teachers who are working in Nursery, than for those in Reception classes. As children move through Nursery into Reception, there is an expectation that they will 'learn to read' and that this reading relates largely to the decoding of print. What is more, in order to teach children 'how to read', reading scheme texts are indeed widely used within early years education (Solity and Vousden, 2009). Yet The Oakfield Study strongly indicated that reading scheme texts were highly instrumental in not only narrowing children's definitions of reading, but in discouraging many of these children from attempting to read books at all. The next section therefore examines how the acquisition of print literacy can be addressed within the Foundation Stage and the implications of this for the use of reading scheme texts.

Print reading and the use of reading scheme texts

Over the years there has been, and there still continues to be, much contention surrounding the subject of teaching children to decode print. The teaching of phonics has been regarded as both an essential element of primary schooling and an activity that is little short of child abuse! Yet there is nothing inherently hazardous about print, or teaching children how to make sense of print. However, serious and justified concerns about the ways in which children are exposed to print in school do indeed exist. As The Oakfield Study confirmed, the ability to decode print has been allowed to shape children's perceptions of themselves as readers, and subsequently cause some children to lose confidence in their own abilities to read *from Nursery onwards*. This alarming fact must be addressed if we are to improve children's attitudes and confidence in reading during their primary years in school.

As this chapter has stressed, though the prescriptive nature of the Foundation Curriculum may place unwelcome constraints upon early years practitioners, there are many ways in which teachers can still present a holistic view of reading that retains a concern for children's confidence and motivations in reading. It is therefore argued here that those teaching within the Foundation Stage can, and indeed should, introduce print to children within meaningful contexts. For example, teachers can structure play-based activity that includes exposure to print. Given that an ability to decode print is a useful strategy to own in making sense of texts, then children should be made aware of this. However, there are two crucial issues that must be acknowledged. Firstly, it is important that the decoding of print is presented as being one of many strategies that can be used to make sense of texts and that it can be used in conjunction with other meaning-making strategies such as sound, picture, moving image and so on. As highlighted in Chapter 5, there is now substantial evidence to support the view that the ways in which print literacy is taught in schools needs to be reconsidered in the light of changing technologies (Turbill, 2002; Hassett, 2006). Teachers of young children today are therefore in the unique and enviable position of being able to observe how the young children they are working with use print within the context of screen texts and multimedia. This knowledge can then be used to help children make sense of print within other contexts, such as paper texts. As this builds upon children's existing experiences, this can also help teachers to promote the view that print is meaningful and useful and should not be viewed with apprehension.

This brings us to the second issue that is important to stress with regard to the teaching of print literacy in the Foundation Stage. While some children clearly enjoy learning to decode print, and see themselves as successful readers because of this, The Oakfield Study indicated that many other children may be developing negative perceptions of themselves from their earliest years in school because they believe that reading is about decoding print, yet they view themselves as unable to fulfil this expectation. This suggests that the Foundation Stage should be a time when children are introduced to print, alongside other meaning-making strategies, in a manner that is free from proficiency grading. In other words, the ability to decode print should not be allowed to define children's perceptions of themselves as readers during these formative years. Without doubt, this does offer a real challenge to early years practitioners. Yet, it is clearly important that teachers develop the ability to carefully reflect on the ways in which they talk about print with their children. By asking questions of themselves, teachers can develop an ability to critically reflect on the ways in which they present print, and the decoding of print, to the children in their class. For example, teachers may ask: *Does my own use of certain terminology suggest that reading is synonymous with decoding print? Do I imply that being unable to decode print means that an individual is unable to read? Do I talk about decoding print in a manner that suggests it is a difficult activity? Are issues of proficiency grading implicit in the ways in which I talk about print with the children in my class?*

Clearly, an ability to critically reflect on such aspects of practice is a crucial step in helping children to develop confidence in handling print. However, The Oakfield Study revealed that there was a specific aspect of reading instruction that seemed to cause particular problems for some children learning to read print during their Foundation Stage years; this related to the use of reading scheme texts. As discussed in Chapter 4, for most of the children in the study, reading schemes appeared to do little to promote meaningful engagement and enjoyment of texts, as most of the children in the study viewed the scheme as merely a tool to teach the mechanics of the decoding skill. Moreover, given that all of the children in the study seemed to think that reading was largely defined as the ability to decode print in reading scheme texts, the scheme promoted a narrow definition of reading. Finally, the reading scheme was seen to be constraining for most of the children in the study, but especially for those who were taking longer to progress through the stages of the scheme. As many of the children reported that they were not 'readers' until they had completed all of the stages of the scheme and were 'on chapter books', being on the scheme appeared to convey the message to the children that they were 'non-readers'. Therefore, the positioning within the scheme seemed to reinforce some children's negative perceptions of themselves as readers, and in some cases was seen to discourage children from attempting to read anything outside of the scheme because they did not believe that they had the necessary reading skills to do so.

This is sound evidence to suggest that practitioners and policy makers must recognise that reading schemes, and indeed similar classificatory reading systems, must be used with extreme caution in early years settings. However, to simply suggest that reading schemes should not be used at all within early years settings would be to somewhat miss the point. Rather, by reflecting on how exactly reading schemes were perceived by the children, much more can be learned about the ways in which practitioners can prevent children from developing negative attitudes towards reading during the Foundation Stage.

Firstly, it was clear that a number of children viewed themselves as 'non-readers' while working through the scheme, as they believed they could only be defined as a 'reader' once they had completed all of the stages on the scheme and were 'on chapter books'. This suggests that practitioners need to work closely with parents and carers to help promote the view that all reading is authentic and valuable. If children, and indeed parents too for that matter, believe that the reading of scheme texts is not 'real' reading, but is simply a programme of training for the future, then it is easy to see how this reading becomes devalued in the eyes of the children. What is more, given the amount of time that many young children are expected to spend reading scheme texts at home and at school, it must be very disheartening to invest so much time and effort into an activity that is simply preparatory and not regarded as 'real' in itself! This again confirms many of the assertions that have already been presented in this book. Rather than presenting young children with a narrow discourse on reading, that suggests to them that learning to read is all about learning to decode print (and in many cases this is within the context of reading scheme texts), children need to be encouraged to value *all* of the reading that they engage with. Moreover, given that parents often look to the school for guidance on how their children should be learning to read, this again demonstrates the importance of home–school communication within early years. While extending communication practices between home and school can help practitioners to understand more about the kind of texts that are meaningful and important to the children in their class, such dialogue also allows teachers to encourage parents to value the variety of reading practices their children may engage with at home.

Secondly, these findings do have major implications for the ways in which reading scheme texts are presented to children in schools and at home. While it must be recognised that there are benefits in having scheme texts (for example, it may be useful for a practitioner to know roughly which stage a child is on in order to plan future activity), it is imperative that the scheme is not allowed to define children's perceptions of themselves as readers. There appears to be very little benefit, and in some cases substantial danger, in children coming to believe that they are only able to read books that are of a particular level in their reading scheme. This may not only create negative self-perceptions in children, but can actively discourage some children from attempting to read books outside of the scheme – or even books of a different level within the scheme. For this reason, if reading schemes are used in Reception then it is highly recommended that they are used in conjunction with many other texts, including a wide variety of fiction and non-fiction books. Moreover, it is also strongly suggested that if they are used, less emphasis is given to the staging within the scheme and more emphasis is allowed to fall on the actual book itself and its intrinsic value as a text. Finally, it seems especially important that if children are reading scheme books at school, or taking them home to read to parents and carers, they are encouraged to view this reading as authentic and as being just as valuable as the reading of other books outside of the scheme.

This section has outlined a number of implications for practice with regard to teaching print literacy within the Foundation Stage. In brief, it is proposed that practitioners embed the acquisition of print literacy into a broad and holistic definition of reading, and that they encourage children to engage with print alongside a variety of other strategies in order to make sense of texts at home and at school. The aim should be that print is neither feared nor disliked, but rather that it is valued as one of the many sign and symbol systems that readers use to enjoy and make sense of texts. Of course, as this book has highlighted on numerous occasions, young children are exposed to a wide variety of texts in modern society which includes access to digital texts and new media. The final section of this chapter therefore examines some of the implications for practice which arise as a result of children's interactions with such media.

Digital texts and new technologies

By maintaining a focus on the role of the teacher in early education settings, this chapter has examined a variety of implications for practice on the basis of various issues raised in this book. Teachers have been urged to reflect on aspects of their practice and consider ways in which they can encourage young children to develop greater confidence in themselves as readers from the Foundation Stage onwards. As stated, given the impact of digital technology within contemporary life (Cope and Kalantzis, 2000; Lankshear and Knobel, 2003), teachers do need to acknowledge its role within reading and literacy education.

However, given that this chapter has argued strongly that definitions of reading must become more holistic and integrated if early years educators are to find ways in which to develop young children's confidence in reading, it would seem a little self-defeating to now suggest that the reading of digital texts should be regarded in isolation from paper texts. Rather, it appears that teachers must recognise that children entering the formal education system are likely to have been exposed to a variety of digital media in their homes (Marsh et al., 2005; Bearne et al., 2007) and that they can capitalise on this experience in order to support children in becoming confident and competent readers of a variety of screen and paper texts. In a recent review of research into technology and early childhood settings, Burnett (2010) concluded that it is now apparent that 'complex interactions ... occur between children, technology, and their wide-ranging experiences of literacy'. Once again, the focus seems to fall on this issue of 'interaction', which suggests that schools must allow for such complex interactions to manifest themselves.

More specifically though, this issue is discussed further in the work of Prensky (2009) who speaks of the concept of children developing 'digital wisdom', i.e. the capacity to capitalise on the rapidly changing landscape of technology and use it 'wisely'. Prensky argues that in order to succeed in the future, humans will need to 'intelligently combine their innate capacities with their digital enhancements' (2009: 3). In this respect, Prensky appears to be suggesting that rather than focusing on the specific ways in which children become competent users of digital technology, it is important to focus on the relationship between cognition and digital media.

While it is not the purpose of this book to explore the specific ways in which individuals develop 'digital wisdom', Prensky's assertion that practitioners should focus on the relationships children develop between their existing understandings of text and their interactions with digital media is important. Once again, this provides further support for the claim that in order for early years practitioners to help children to become competent and confident users of text, then they need to view the relationship between traditional and digital media as reciprocal and mutually supportive. In other words, this suggests that for practitioners to encourage children to develop strong relationships with text, they must not only include exposure to digital technologies in the classroom, but must actively encourage children to build on the skills and strategies they develop in their homes to make sense of digital texts and use these within all aspects of their reading.

☐ Summary

This chapter has presented an outline of the ways in which practitioners working in early years education can support children's confidence in themselves as readers. Drawing on findings from The Oakfield Study, these recommendations for practice focus very much on the ways in which teachers can promote holistic and inclusive definitions of reading in the classroom that show that they value a wide variety of strategies to make sense of texts. Much of this is dependent upon fostering relationships between parents, teachers, children and various reading texts and practices. As this chapter has stressed, in order for teachers to develop holistic definitions of reading, there is a need for them to enter into the learning situation which is taking place alongside the children. There is also a need for teachers to extend communication practices with parents and carers in order to gain an understanding of what is significant for their children, and thus create opportunities in school for children to interact with texts and develop strategies to make sense of texts within contexts that are meaningful. What is more, communication with children's parents and carers will also allow teachers to encourage parents to show their children that they too value the variety of reading practices that children engage with in their homes.

This chapter has further recommended that teachers find creative and meaningful ways in which to expose young children to print and opportunities for children to build upon their own experiences of handling print in their homes. However, it has been stressed that print reading should be introduced to children as one of the many strategies that can be used to make sense of a range of texts. Moreover, this chapter has also warned that the ability to decode print should not be allowed to shape children's perceptions of themselves as readers during their initial years in school.

This has a particular salience for the use of reading scheme texts which have been seen to endorse negative self-perceptions in young children and actually discourage some children from reading at all. This chapter has recommended that if reading schemes are used within the Foundation Curriculum, teachers should ensure that the use of the scheme does not prevent children from seeing themselves as readers. It is also recommended that these texts are used alongside a wide variety of other book and screen texts and that teachers ensure that there is less of an emphasis on the books as a staged system and more on the actual value of the whole book as a text.

As this book comes to a close, it is hoped that teachers and practitioners working with young children today do find that they are indeed able to look beyond the targets and aims of the current reading curriculum and find their own ways in which to promote meaningful engagement with texts in the classroom. Of course, what would make the task easier would be a change in the curriculum to afford teachers more time and opportunity to implement the recommendations presented in this book. The concluding chapter now turns to the issue of policy and presents recommendations for a change in the reading curriculum within the Foundation Stage. Implications of this work for future research are also discussed in this conclusion.

Key questions

- How can aspects of classroom practice, and the creation of the classroom environment, transmit judgements about 'what counts' as reading?
- How can teachers situate reading education within a playful discourse?
- What can teachers do to show that they are entering the learning experience with children?

Conclusion

By maintaining a focus on the voices of children themselves, this book has provided an insight into the ways in which young children develop perceptions of reading and has explained how these perceptions can have a profound influence on children's confidence and motivations for reading. As a consequence, this book has exposed many of the complex issues surrounding the teaching and learning of reading as young children enter the formal schooling system.

On the basis of findings from research, this book has offered a number of suggestions for teachers and early years practitioners working with young children in educational settings. In particular, the previous chapter invited teachers to reflect critically on aspects of their practice and find their own ways in which to encourage young children to develop positive and useful perceptions of reading. Rather than providing teachers with a template for teaching reading, this book has encouraged teachers to consider how factors such as their own perceptions of reading may have a bearing on how young children come to formulate beliefs and attitudes towards reading. Moreover, the previous chapter also recommended that teachers consider how factors such as the role of play and the development of various relationships, such as the teacher–pupil relationship, can influence children's perceptions of reading.

While it is perfectly possible for teachers to engage with these concepts within the context of the existing Foundation Curriculum, what is really required is change at the level of policy. Indeed the New Brunswick Curriculum Framework for Early Learning and Child Care, developed by the Early Childhood Research and Development Team (2008) and recently implemented in Canada, provides an excellent example of a curriculum for children aged 5 and under that truly acknowledges the uniqueness of children within its philosophy for teaching and learning. Given that this book has demonstrated that the school discourse on reading is highly influential in shaping young children's perceptions of reading and in developing their confidence in themselves as readers, the objectives which drive the implementation of the Foundation Curriculum must be given careful consideration. Using the New Brunswick Curriculum Framework as a model, this concluding chapter therefore provides suggestions for changes in policy which determine the curriculum for young children within the Foundation

Stage. This chapter also offers suggestions for future research to develop further and deeper understandings of children's literacy learning.

A Foundation Curriculum: promoting confidence in reading

The New Brunswick Curriculum Framework has been chosen as a model upon which to frame this discussion because the objectives at the heart of the curriculum closely correspond with many of the issues and implications raised in this book. For example, it is documented that the curriculum has been designed with this vision in mind:

> In keeping with contemporary research and theory, the framework emphasizes responsive relationships, children's strengths, and engaging environments. It views children as confident, active learners whose learning, growth, and development are profoundly influenced by the quality of their relationships with people and their interactions with places and things. (Section 1: 1)

There are several issues to consider here in terms of developing curriculum guidance for the teaching of children aged 5 and under. Firstly, this curriculum is grounded within a concern for theory that acknowledges relevant findings from contemporary research. Indeed, it has been strongly argued in this book that policy makers must recognise that research has indicated that many young children appear to be developing negative perceptions of themselves as readers as a direct consequence of the schooling of reading. It therefore seems imperative that those involved in the design of an early years curriculum ensure that the content of the curriculum is based upon sound evidence gained from rigorous research into various aspects of young children's reading. Secondly, it is important that this research includes study that has been devoted to accessing the voices of young children themselves and attempts to understand issues of confidence and motivation in reading. Only then can policy makers begin to develop a curriculum that meets the needs of young children as they enter the formal education system today.

A third issue relates to the conceptualisation of children and childhood that is presented in this statement. A crucial term to acknowledge is the concept of children being 'active learners'. As raised in the previous chapter, it has been suggested that in order to encourage young children to value and feel at liberty to build on the strategies they develop at home and at school to make sense of texts, teachers of young children need to enter into the learning situation with the children. In doing so, teachers will be able to encourage children to develop their own relationships with learning, which is vital if children are to develop motivations for reading. However, it is clearly the case that the structure of the current Foundation Curriculum provides little opportunity for teachers to enter into such relationships with children, due to the target-driven nature of the curriculum.

Given this assertion, it is not surprising that the vision statement quoted above contains multiple references to the development of relationships. Indeed, as this book has repeatedly demonstrated, there are a variety of relationships that need to be cultivated within the early years setting in order to promote confidence and motivation for reading. As mentioned, these include the teacher–pupil relationship, practitioner's relationships with parents/carers, children's relationships with texts and children's relationship with learning. But how can this be achieved? Again, we can turn to the New Brunswick Curriculum Framework for suggestions.

The New Brunswick Curriculum Framework essentially contains four broad goals for early learning and care: *Well-being*; *Play and Playfulness*; *Communication and Literacies*; and *Diversity and Social Responsibility*. Yet these goals are very much situated within a wider ethos that is explicitly value based, rather than target driven. At the heart of the curriculum is a desire to value children, value culture and languages, value relationships and value environments. Therefore, the four goals for early learning and care cannot be separated from these intrinsic values. As a consequence, this curriculum succeeds in being truly holistic, promoting the view that for young children learning should be about building connections and developing relationships, rather than achieving attainment targets.

Moreover, it is clearly the case that not only do these values resonate throughout the entire curriculum, but the goals are themselves mutually dependent. For example, within the description of the goal for *Well-being* is the aim to 'promote a zest for living and learning' (Section 2: 20). In other words, teachers are being encouraged to prioritise children's own relationships with learning as a fundamental learning objective. This is echoed throughout the document and features within all other descriptions of learning objectives. What is more, the document states that children should 'invent symbols and develop systems of representation' within the goal of *Play and Playfulness*. This objective is then reaffirmed in the *Communication and Literacies* goal, which includes multimodal meaning making as a central focus, and promotes the view that children should engage with a variety of sign systems and interact with symbols and practices of language, maths, art and drama.

This book has argued that for many young children in the Foundation Stage of schooling, there is an urgent need for schools to find ways in which to promote reading as a holistic and engaging activity. Based on research findings, as discussed in this book, it is clear that schools must offer a broader discourse on reading that allows young children to develop a range of skills to make sense of a variety of texts and symbolic systems. It has been strongly argued that educators must promote reading as an enjoyable, interactive activity that is situated within a playful and meaningful discourse. Certainly, the New Brunswick Curriculum Framework offers clear guidance as to the ways in which factors such as the facilitative role of play and a concern to build strong relationships can indeed drive a foundation curriculum for young children.

In Section 4 of the document, practitioners are presented with a detailed expansion of the four learning goals, which provides a range of suggestions for practice, based upon the values already described. This means that for the goal *Communication and Literacies*, suggestions for practice make specific reference to the values described above. Heading this section, for the expansion of the *Communication and Literacies* goal, is the overall aim that:

> Children experience intellectually, socially and culturally engaging environments where their communicative practices, languages and literacies and literate identities are valued and supported. (Section 4: 123)

First and foremost, it is highly gratifying to see that the commitment to value and support children's literate identities sits as a fundamental objective of the literacy curriculum. As this book has highlighted, it is clearly the case that schools must find ways in which to show young children that their home literacy practices are indeed valued in school, and that there is space in school for these practices, skills and strategies to be supported and enhanced. By situating a concern for the preservation of children's own literate identities at the heart of the literacy curriculum, practitioners will be more able to construct and engage in activities that support children's confidence in themselves as readers.

Secondly, the specific learning objectives within the *Communication and Literacies* component of the curriculum also connect with many of the recommendations that have emerged from this book. For example, the document states (see Section 4: 123) that a focus should fall on children:

- forming relationships through communicative practice

- learning the conventions of their languages

- extending ideas and taking action through language

- exploring a variety of sign systems

- engaging in multimodal meaning making

- co-constructing a range of literate identities

- engaging critically in the literacy practices of popular culture

- using the literacy tools of digital technology.

It must be recognised that as this curriculum has been devised to meet the specific needs of children in the New Brunswick area, any changes to the existing Foundation Curriculum would equally need to reflect the needs of children growing up within a UK context. However, it must be further acknowledged that not only has the New Brunswick Curriculum Framework been developed on the basis of sound research and theoretical foundations, it also strongly correlates with many of the issues raised in this book. For example, it has been argued in this book that a reading curriculum for children within the Foundation Stage of schooling should recognise and accommodate the shifts in reading practices that have occurred as a result of children's engagement with popular culture and digital texts. The New Brunswick Curriculum Framework has succeeded in developing a curriculum that does indeed reflect such changes in textual landscape, while simultaneously acknowledging that reading and literacy practices are grounded in a variety of multimodal skills that include abilities to make sense of a range of symbol systems including print. For these reasons, it is highly recommended that those involved in the process of constructing a curriculum for children in the Foundation Stage consider the benefits of implementing a values-based curriculum such as this in order to ensure that early years practitioners are given the opportunities that they require to focus on children's confidence and motivation for reading during these early years in school.

Assessment

This book has warned that various modes of assessment operating within the existing curriculum can be deeply discouraging for some children learning to read in schools today. In particular, the use of reading scheme texts has been seen to induce proficiency judgements that can have a negative effect on children's confidence, and in some cases even discourage children from reading. While it has been recommended that practitioners take care to ensure that reading schemes are not allowed to dominate children's perceptions of their proficiency in reading, this raises questions about how the assessment of reading can influence young children's views of themselves as readers and their motivation to tackle a variety of texts with independence. Moreover, if the early years reading curriculum were to become more value led, as suggested, with issues of confidence and motivation driving its development, then the assessment of this curriculum must also reflect these concerns.

But how could such a curriculum be assessed? This can be something of a challenge, especially given the multimodal nature of children's reading practices today. Bearne et al. (2007) discovered that young screen readers between the ages of 3 and 16 were using a range of skills and strategies to access meaning, many of which could be described by the QCA (now QCDA – Qualifications and Assessment Development Agency) reading assessment focuses. Yet they also point out that there are certain features of multimodal reading that current assessment focuses cannot describe. They state:

> Children's multimodal compositions, by their very nature, cannot be assessed in the same way as paper texts. The same is true of multimodal reading. The reading assessment focuses cannot capture the interpretation of sound, movement and colour as part of the reading process. (2007: 20)

Bearne et al. go on to stress that many further aspects of children's screen reading, such as the ability to become a discriminating or diverse screen reader, cannot be covered within the assessment focuses. This suggests that given the change in textual landscape, it may be time to re-evaluate the role of assessment altogether within the early years reading curriculum. However, that is not to say that children should not be assessed; rather, policy makers need to consider how reading assessment can be most usefully employed within the curriculum.

To turn attention once again to the New Brunswick Curriculum Framework (Section 3), they have implemented two strands of assessment: 'narrative' and 'normative'. Narrative assessment is described as an illustrative form of assessment, based upon illustration, description and interpretation of children's learning. It is argued that this form of assessment 'builds community and links children's learning to curricular goals and future planning' (Section 4: 63). In other words, the document is suggesting that through careful listening and observation, practitioners can learn much about children's interests and strengths so as to plan appropriately for individuals and small groups of children. The second mode of assessment (normative) is described as an individual assessment that locates development in relation to age-group norms, such as milestones. However, the document warns that 'this form of assessment must be used carefully and thoughtfully, keeping in mind that all norms are socially and culturally biased' (Section 4: 63).

Crucially, these modes of assessment are both used as part of the wider curricular objectives to help maintain healthy relationships with children, families and colleagues. It is argued that assessment should be conducted to help educators plan children's learning, but also to help maintain communicative relationships with children and their families. However, it is further stressed that such assessment is time consuming and cannot be achieved unless educators are provided with sufficient non-contact time to reflect on the assessments and plan to meet the needs of children in the light of this.

Finally, the New Brunswick Curriculum Framework makes the point that assessment should also include having opportunities to reflect on the effectiveness of the curriculum and finding ways in which to improve practice. While this is certainly laudable, it is of course very difficult to promote changes in policy on the basis of reflection upon individual practice. This brings us back to the role of research. As stated at the beginning of this chapter, policy must be guided by contemporary and high quality research. This book has described various ways in which early years reading instruction can be guided by research findings. However, this is by no means the end of the story. This final section now reflects upon the findings from The Oakfield Study and describes the implications of these for future research.

Future research

This book has shown that as new aspects of media and digital technology continue to impact upon the reading repertoires of children today, even the youngest of children are capable of embracing these changes with competence and enthusiasm. Yet it is clear that schools need to recognise these changes and find ways in which to help children to develop into confident users of text. A number of recommendations for changes in practice and policy have been presented in this book, but it would be a mistake to believe that we now understand young children's perceptions of reading.

On the contrary, the research presented in this book indicates that there is still much to be learned about the ways in which young children interact with texts at home and school. Moreover, it is also clear that if teachers are to accommodate children's digital and screen-reading practices in schools, then there is an urgent need to understand more about how children read such texts and the implications of this for their wider attitudes towards reading in general. As reading practices continue to shift and develop in line with changes in technology, research must also continue to focus on how children use such texts and the implications of this for reading instruction.

Having discovered, through the context of The Oakfield Study, that children's perceptions of reading are highly influenced by issues of proficiency judgement, further research must now broaden this focus to include writing as well as reading. Further study must now explore the ways in which the schooling of literacy has an impact upon young children's attitudes towards literacy and their perceptions of themselves as users of language.

Moreover, having established that the school discourse plays a vital role in shaping young children's perceptions of themselves as readers, it seems to be of importance that we now understand the ways in which the school discourse moulds children's perceptions of themselves within other contexts. For example, how does the schooling of other subjects influence children's perceptions of themselves as writers, mathematicians or musicians for example? Moreover, given the attitudes of some of the children described in The Oakfield Study, and the factors that influenced the formation of these attitudes, it now seems to be of huge importance that we understand how the school setting can influence young children's perceptions of themselves as learners and as members of the school community.

Finally, much of this proposed research continues to be dependent on the ability to access quality data from very young children. It is hoped that the research presented in this book, and in relation to The Oakfield

Study in particular, will help other researchers to develop skills, strategies and resources to access the voices of young children within participatory research such as this.

Conclusion

Through an insight into the thoughts and perceptions of young children, this book has illustrated the complexities and challenges facing young children today as they learn to read. Yet this is a challenge that we must face. This book has shown that schools can be responsible for discouraging some young children from becoming confident readers of texts, yet it has also been stressed that there is a vast amount that we, as educators of young children, can do to promote confidence in handling and reading texts. By recognising the uniqueness of each child, as well as the impact of our role as early years educators, we can do much to guide children in the path of becoming confident and capable users of texts. But most of all, we can help children to experience the pleasure of engaging with the diversity of texts available within modern society and encourage a motivation for reading that will last a lifetime.

List of references

Adams, M.J. (1990) *Beginning to read: Thinking and learning about print*. Cambridge, MA: MIT Press.

Anning, A. (2003) 'Pathways to the graphicacy club: The crossroad of home and pre-school', *Journal of Early Childhood Literacy*, 3 (1): 5–35.

Arizpe, E. and Styles, M. (2003) *Children Reading Pictures: Interpreting visual texts*. London: RoutledgeFalmer.

Arthur, L. (2005) 'Popular culture: Views of parents and educators', in J. Marsh (ed.), *Popular Culture, New Media and Digital Literacy in Early Childhood*. London: RoutledgeFalmer. pp. 165–82.

Australian Government Department Of Education, Science and Training (2005) *Teaching Reading. Report and Recommendations. National Enquiry into the Teaching of Literacy*. Barton, Australia: Department of Education, Science and Training.

Barlow, J.P. (1996) 'A Declaration of the Independence of Cyberspace'. Available: https://projects.eff.org/~barlow/Declaration-Final.html. (Accessed 11 November 2010).

Beard, R. (2003) 'Uncovering the key skills of reading', in N. Hall, J. Larson and J. Marsh (eds), *Handbook of Early Childhood Literacy*. London: Sage. pp. 199–208.

Bearne, E. (2003) 'Rethinking literacy: communication, representation and text', *Reading Literacy and Language*, 37 (3): 98–103.

Bearne, E. (2004) 'Multimodal texts: what they are and how children use them', in J. Evans (ed.), *New ways of Reading, New Ways of Writing: Using Popular Culture, New Technologies and Critical Literacy in the Primary Classroom*. New York: Heinemann. pp. 16–30.

Bearne, E. and Marsh, J. (eds) (2007) *Literacy and social inclusion: Closing the gap*. Stoke on Trent: Trentham.

Bearne, E., Clark, C., Johnson, A., Manford, P., Mottram, M. and Wolstencroft, H. (2007) *Reading on Screen*. Leicester: UKLA.

Behrendt, S.C. (1996) 'Reader and texts in the eighteenth-century illustrated book: illustrations as teachers', in W.F. Garrett-Petts and D. Lawrence (eds), *Integrating Visual and Verbal Literacies*. Winnipeg: Inkshed Publications. pp. 39–52.

Bennett, S., Maton, K. and Kervin, L. (2008) 'The "digital natives" debate: A critical review of the evidence', *British Journal of Educational Technology*, 39 (5): 775–86.

BERA (2004) *Revised Ethical Guidelines for Educational Research*. Available: www.bera.ac.uk/files/guidelines/ethical.pdf. (Accessed 11 November 2010).

Bernstein, B. (1971) *Class, Codes and Control*. London: Routledge and Kegan Paul.

Bhabha, H.K. (1994) *The Location of Culture*. New York: Routledge.

Bloodgood, J.W. (1999) '"What's in a name?" Children's name writing and literacy acquisition', *Reading Research Quarterly*, 34 (3): 342–67.

Bonnett, M. (1994) *Children's Thinking*. London: Cassell.

Brenna, B. (1995) 'The metacognitive reading strategies of five early readers', *Journal of Research in Reading*, 18 (1): 53–62.

Bronfenbrenner, U. (1979) *The Ecology of Human Development*. Massachusetts: Harvard University Press.

Brooker, L. (2002) *Starting school – Young Children Learning Cultures*. Buckingham: Open University Press.

Burnett, C. (2010) 'Technology and literacy in early childhood educational settings: a review of research', *Journal of Early Childhood Literacy*, 10 (3): 247–70.

Byrnes, J.P. and Wasik, B.A. (2009) *Literacy and Language development: what educators need to know*. New York: The Guilford Press.

Cairney, T. (2003) 'Literacy within family life', in N. Hall, J. Larson and J. Marsh (eds), *Handbook of Early Childhood Literacy*. London: Sage. pp. 85–98.

Campbell, R. (1992) *Reading Real Books*. Buckingham: Open University Press.

Carrington, V. (2005) 'New textual landscapes, information and early literacy', in J. Marsh (ed.), *Popular Culture, New Media and Digital Literacy in Early Childhood*. Abingdon: RoutledgeFalmer. pp. 13–27.

Comaskey, E., Savage, R. and Abrami, P.C. (2009) 'A randomized efficacy study of web-based synthetic and analytic programmes among disadvantaged urban kindergarten children', *Journal of Research in Reading*, 32 (1): 92–108.

Compton-Lilly, C. (2006) 'Identity, childhood culture and literacy learning: A case study', *Journal of Early Childhood Literacy*, 6 (1): 57–76.

Cook, M. (2005) '"A place of their own": creating a classroom "third space" to support a continuum of text construction between home and school', *Literacy*, 39 (2): 85–90.

Cope, B. and Kalantzis, M. (2000) *Multiliteracies: Literacy learning and the design of social futures*. London: Routledge.

Cremin, H. and Slatter, B. (2004) 'Is it possible to access the "voice" of pre-school children? Results of a research project in a pre-school setting', *Educational Studies*, 30 (4): 457–70.

Crowther, J., Hamilton, M. and Tett, L. (2001) *Powerful Literacies*. Leicester: NIACE.

Department for Education (2010) *Statutory Framework for EYFS: Learning and development requirements*. Available: http://www.nationalstrategies.standards.dcsf.gov.uk/eyfs/site/requirements/leaning/goals.htm. (Accessed 11 November 2010).

Department for Education and Employment (DfEE) (1998) *The National Literacy Strategy: a framework for teaching*. London: HMSO.

Department for Education and Employment (DfEE) (2001) *Watching and learning 2: OISE/UT evaluation of the implementation of the National Literacy and Numeracy Strategies*. London: HMSO.

Department for Education and Science (DES) (1975) *A language for life*. London: HMSO.

Department for Education and Skills (DfES) (1998) *Progression in Phonics: materials for whole-class teaching*. London: Department for Education and Employment.

Department for Education and Skills (DfES) (2003) *Teaching phonics in the NLS*. London: HMSO.

Department for Education and Skills (DfES) (2004) *Playing with sounds*. London: Department for Education and Employment.

Department for Education and Skills (DfES) (2007) *Letters and Sounds: Principles and practice of high quality phonics*. London: Department for Education and Employment.

Donaldson, M. (1978) *Children's minds*. Glasgow: Fontana.

Dyson, A.H. (1997) *Writing Superheroes: Contemporary Childhood, Popular Culture and Classroom Literacy*. New York: Teachers College Press.

Early Childhood Research and Development Team (2008) *New Brunswick Curriculum Framework for Early Learning and Child Care*. New Brunswick: Department of Social Development.

Facer, K., Furlong, J., Furlong, R. and Sutherland, R. (2003) *Screenplay: Children and computing in the home*. London: RoutledgeFalmer.

France, A. (2004) 'Young people', in S. Fraser, V. Lewis, S. Ding, M. Kellett and C. Robinson (eds), *Doing Research with Children and Young People*. London: Sage. pp. 175–90.

Garrett-Petts, W.F. (2000) 'Garry Disher, Michael Ondaatje, and the haptic eye: taking a second look at print literacy', *Children's Literature in Education*, 31 (1): 39–52.

Garvey, C. (1977) *Play*. London: Fontana.

Glister, P. (1997) *Digital Literacy*. New York: John Wiley and Sons.

Goodman, K. (1986) *What's Whole in Whole Language?* Portsmouth: Heinemann.

Goodwin, P. (2008) *Understanding children's books: A guide for education professionals*. London: Sage.

Gough, P.B. and Hillinger, M.L. (1980) 'Learning to read: An unusual act', *Bulletin of the Orton Society*, 30: 179–96.

Greig, A. and Taylor, J. (1999) *Doing Research with Children*. London: Sage.

Hall, C. and Coles, M. (1997) 'Gendered readings: helping boys develop as critical readers', *Gender and Education*, 9 (1): 61–8.

Hall, C. and Coles, M. (1999) *Children's Reading Choices*. London: Routledge.

Hall, K. (2003) *Listening to Stephen Read: Multiple perspectives on literacy*. Buckingham: Open University Press.

Hannon, P. and James, S. (1990) 'Parents' and teachers' perspectives on pre-school literacy development', *British Educational Research Journal*, 16 (3): 259–72.

Hare, W. (1992) 'Humility as a virtue in teaching', *Journal of Philosophy in Education*, 26 (2): 227–36.

Hassett, D.D. (2006) 'Signs of the times: the governance of alphabetic print over "appropriate" and "natural" reading development', *Journal of Early Childhood Literacy*, 6 (1): 77–103.

Heath, S.B. (1983) *Ways with Words: Language, Life and Work in Communities and Classrooms*. Cambridge: Cambridge University Press.

Holloway, S.L. and Valentine, G. (2003) *Cyberkids: Children in the information age*. London: RoutledgeFalmer.

Horner, S.L. and O'Connor, E.A. (2007) 'Helping beginning and struggling readers to develop self-regulated strategies: A reading recovery example', *Reading and Writing Quarterly*, 23 (1): 97–109.

Isaacs, S. (1930) *Intellectual growth in young children*. London: Routledge and Kegan Paul.

Jones, N. (1990) 'Reader, Writer, Text', in R. Carter (ed.), *Knowledge about Language and the Curriculum*. London: Hodder and Stoughton.

Kellett, M. and Ding, S. (2004) 'Middle Childhood', in S. Fraser, V. Lewis, S. Ding, M. Kellett and C. Robinson (eds), *Doing Research with Children and Young People*. London: Sage. pp. 161–74.

Kirby, J.R. and Savage, R.S. (2008) 'Can the simple view deal with the complexities of reading?' Literacy, 42 (2): 75–82.

Knobel, M. and Lankshear, C. (2003) 'Researching young children's out-of-school literacy practices', in N. Hall, J. Larson and J. Marsh (eds), Handbook of Early Childhood Literacy. London: Sage. pp. 51–65.

Kress, G. (1997) Before writing – rethinking the paths to literacy. London: Routledge.

Kress, G. (2000) 'Multimodality', in B. Cope and M. Kalantzis (eds), Multiliteracies: Literacy, Learning and the Design of Social Futures. London: Routledge. pp. 179–200.

Kress, G. and van Leeuwen, T. (1996) The Grammar of Visual Design. London: Routledge.

Kress, G. and van Leeuwen, T. (2001) Multimodal discourse: The modes and media of contemporary communication. London: Cassell.

Lankshear, C. and Knobel, M. (2003) New literacies: Changing knowledge and class-room learning. Milton Keynes: Open University Press.

Levy, R. (2008) '"Third spaces" are interesting places; applying "third space theory" to nursery-aged children's constructions of themselves as readers', Journal of Early Childhood Literacy, 8 (1): 43–66.

Levy, R. (2009a) '"You have to understand words … but not read them": young children becoming readers in a digital age', Journal of Research in Reading, 32 (1): 75–91.

Levy, R. (2009b) 'Children's perceptions of reading and the use of reading scheme texts', Cambridge Journal of Education, 39 (3): 361–77.

Lewis, D. (2001) 'Showing and telling: the difference that makes a difference', Reading Literacy and Language, 35 (3): 94–8.

Luke, A., Carrington, V. and Kapitzke, C. (2003) 'Textbooks and early childhood literacy', in N. Hall, J. Larson and J. Marsh (eds), Handbook of Early Childhood Literacy. London: Sage. pp. 249–57.

Luke, A. and Freebody, P. (1999–2000) 'Further Notes on the Four Resources Model'. Reading Online. Available: www.readingonline.org/research/lukefreebody.html. (Accessed 11 November 2010).

Lysaker, J.T. (2006) 'Young children's readings of wordless picture books: What's "self" got to do with it?', Journal of Early Childhood Literacy, 6 (1): 33–55.

MacNaughton, G. (2000) Rethinking Gender in Early Childhood Education. London: Paul Chapman.

Makin, L. (2003) 'Creating positive literacy learning environments in early child-hood', in N. Hall, J. Larson and J. Marsh (eds), Handbook of Early Childhood Literacy. London: Sage. pp. 327–37.

Marsh, J. (1999) 'Batman and Batwoman go to school: popular culture in the lit-eracy curriculum,' International Journal of Early Years Education, 7 (2): 117–31.

Marsh, J. (2000) '"But I want to fly too!": girls and superhero play in the infant classroom', Gender and Education, 12 (2): 209–20.

Marsh, J. (2003a) 'Contemporary models of communicative practice: shaky founda-tions in the Foundation Stage', English in Education, 37 (1): 38–46.

Marsh, J. (2003b) 'One-way traffic? Connections between literacy practices at home and in the Nursery', British Educational Research Journal, 29 (3): 369–82.

Marsh, J. (2005) 'Children of the digital age', in J. Marsh (ed.), Popular Culture, New Media and Digital Literacy in Early Childhood. London: RoutledgeFalmer. pp. 1–10.

Marsh, J. (2008) 'Popular culture in the language arts classroom', in J. Flood, S.B. Heath and D. Lapp (eds), *Handbook of Research in the Visual and Creative Arts*, Volume II. New York: MacMillan/IRA.

Marsh, J., Brookes, G., Hughes, J., Ritchie, L., Roberts, S. and Wright, K. (2005) *Digital Beginnings: Young children's use of popular culture, media and new technologies*. Literacy Research Centre, University of Sheffield.

Marsh, J. and Singleton, C. (2009) 'Editorial: Literacy and technology: questions of relationship', *Journal of research in reading*, 32 (1): 1–5.

Martinez, M., Roser, N. and Dooley, C. (2003) 'Young children's literary meaning making', in N. Hall, J. Larson and J. Marsh (eds), *Handbook of early childhood literacy*. London: Sage. pp. 222–34.

McGuinness, D. (2005) *Language Development and Learning to Read*. Massachusetts: The MIT Press.

Meek, M. (1988) *How texts teach what readers learn*. Exeter: The Thimble Press.

Merchant, G. (2007) 'Writing in the future in the digital age', *Literacy*, 41 (3): 118–28.

Millard, E. (1997) *Differently Literate*. London: RoutledgeFalmer.

Millard, E. (2003) 'Gender and early childhood literacy', in N. Hall, J. Larson and J. Marsh (eds) *Handbook of Early Childhood Literacy*. London: Sage. pp. 22–33.

Millard, E. and Marsh, J. (2001) 'Words with pictures: the role of visual literacy in writing and its implication for schooling', *Reading Literacy and Language*, 35 (2): 54–61.

Minns, H. (1997) *Read it to me now!: Learning at home and at school*. Buckingham: Open University Press.

Moje, E.B., Ciechanowski, K.M., Kramer, K., Ellis, L., Carrillo, R. and Collazo, T. (2004) 'Working toward third space in content area literacy: An examination of everyday funds of knowledge and discourse', *Reading Research Quarterly*, 39 (1): 40–70.

Moll, L.C., Amanti, C., Neff, D. and Gonzalez, N. (1992) 'Funds of knowledge for teaching using a qualitative approach to connect homes and classrooms', *Theory into Practice*, 31 (1): 132–41.

Moss, G. (2000) 'Raising boys' attainment in reading: some principles for intervention', *Reading*. 34 (3): 101–6.

Moss, G. (2007) *Literacy and Gender: Researching texts, contexts and readers*. Abingdon: Routledge.

Moyles, J. (1989) *Just playing?: Role and status of play in early childhood education*. Milton Keynes: Open University Press.

National Institute of Child Health and Human Development (NICHHD) (2000) *Report of the national reading panel: Teaching children to read*. pp. 99–176.

NFER (2003) *Progress in International Reading Literacy Study: Reading over the world*. Slough: NFER.

Nicholson, T. (1993) 'Reading without context', in G.B. Thompson, W.E. Tunmer and T. Nicholson (eds), *Reading Acquisition Processes*. Cleveland: Multilingual Matters Ltd. pp. 205–22.

Nikolajeva, M. and Scott, C. (2000) 'The dynamics of picturebook communication', *Children's Literature in Education*, 31 (4): 225–39.

Nutbrown, C. and Hannon, P. (2003) 'Children's perspectives on family literacy: Methodological issues, findings and implications for practice, *Journal of Early Childhood Literacy*, 3 (2): 115–45.

Ofsted (1996) *The teaching of reading in 45 inner London primary schools*. London: Ofsted.

Ofsted (2004) *Reading for purpose and pleasure, an evaluation of the reading in primary schools*. London: Ofsted.

Oritz, R.W. and Stile, S. (1996) 'A preliminary study of fathers' reading activities with their pre-school children from three academic programs: Head start, Developmentally delayed and Gifted. Paper presented at the New Mexico Federation of the Council for Exceptional Children Conference, Albuquerque, New Mexico.

Pahl, K. (2002) 'Ephemera, mess and miscellaneous piles: Texts and practices in families', *Journal of Early Childhood Literacy*, 2 (2): 145–66.

Prensky, M. (2009) 'From digital immigrants and digital natives to digital wisdom'. Available: www.innovateonline.info/pdf/vol5_issue3/H._Sapiens_Digital-__From_ Digital_Immigrants_and_Digital_Natives_to_Digital_Wisdom.pdf. (Accessed 11 November 2010).

Rose, J. (2006) *Independent Review of the Teaching of Early Reading*. Nottingham: DfES.

Roskos, K. and Christie, J. (2001) 'Examining the play-literacy interface: a critical review and future directions', *Journal of Early Childhood Literacy*, 191: 59–89.

Saint-Laurent, L. and Giasson, J. (2005) 'Effects of a family literacy program adapting parental intervention to first graders' evolution of reading and writing abilities', *Journal of Early Childhood Literacy*, 5 (3): 253–78.

Scharer, P.L. and Zutell, J. (2003) 'The development of spelling', in N. Hall, J. Larson and J. Marsh (eds), *Handbook of early childhood literacy*. London: Sage. pp. 271–86.

Scott, J. (2000) 'Children as Respondents', in P. Christensen and A. James (eds), *Research with Children: Perspectives and Practices*. London: Routledge. pp. 98–119.

Smith, E. (2003) 'Failing boys and moral panics: perspectives on the underachievement debate', *British Journal of Educational Studies*, 51 (3): 282–95.

Smith, F. (1971) *Understanding Reading*. London: Holt, Rinehart and Winston.

Smith, F. (1973) *Psycholinguistics and reading*. New York: Holt, Rinehart and Winston.

Smith, F. (1978) *Understanding Reading: A psycholinguistic analysis of reading and learning to read*, 2nd edn. New York/London: Holt, Rinehart and Winston.

Snow, C.E., Burns, M.S. and Griffin, P. (eds) (1998) *Preventing reading difficulties in young children*. Washington DC: National Academy Press.

Solity, J. and Vousden, J. (2009) 'Real books vs reading schemes: a new perspective from instructional psychology', *Educational Psychology*, 29 (4): 469–511.

Stainthorp, R. (2003) 'Phonology and learning to read', in N. Hall, J. Larson and J. Marsh (eds), *Handbook of Early Childhood Literacy*. London: Sage. pp. 209–21.

Stanovich, K.E. (1980) 'Toward an interactive-compensatory model of individual differences in the development of reading fluency', *Reading Research Quarterly*, 16: 32–71.

Stanovich, K.E. and Stanovich, P.J. (1999) 'How research might inform the debate about early reading acquisition', in J. Oakhill and R. Beard (eds), *Reading Development and the Teaching of Reading*. Oxford: Blackwell. pp. 12–41.

Stuart, M., Masterson, J., Dixon, M. and Quinlan, P. (1999) 'Inferring sublexical correspondences from sight vocabulary: Evidence from 6- and 7-year olds', *Quarterly Journal of Experimental Psychology*, 52A: 353–66.

Stuart, M., Stainthorp, R. and Snowling, M. (2008) 'Literacy as a complex activity: deconstructing the simple view of reading', *Literacy*, 42 (1): 60–6.

Tapscott, D. (2009) *Grown Up Digital: How the net generation is changing your world*. New York: McGraw Hill.

Tizard, B. and Hughes, M. (1984) *Young Children Learning: Talking and Thinking at Home and at School*. London: Falmer.

Torgerson, C.J., Brooks, G. and Hall, J. (2006) *A Systematic Review of the Research Literature on the Use of Phonics in the Teaching of Reading and Spelling*. London: Department for Education and Skills (DfES).

Tudge, J.R.H., Odero, D.A., Hogan, D.M. and Etz, K.E. (2003) 'Relations between the everyday activities of pre-schoolers and their teachers' perceptions of their competence in the first years of school', *Early Childhood Research Quarterly*, 18: 42–64.

Turbill, J. (2002, February) 'The four ages of reading philosophy and pedagogy: A framework for examining theory and practice'. Reading Online. Available: www.readingonline.org/international/inter_index.asp?HREF=/international/turbill4/index.html. (Accessed 11 November 2010).

Twist, L., Schagen, I. and Hodgson, C. (2007) *Readers and reading: The national report for England 2006*. Slough, UK: NFER.

UKLA (2006) *Submission to the review of best practice in the teaching of early reading*. Herts: UKLA.

Walsh, M. (2003) 'Reading pictures: what do they reveal? Young children's reading of visual texts,' *Reading Literacy and Language*, 37 (3): 123–30.

Waterland, L. (1985) *Read With Me: An Apprenticeship to Reading*. Gloucestershire: Thimble Press.

Waterman, A., Blades, M. and Spencer, C. (2001) 'Is a jumper angrier than a tree?', *The Psychologist*, 14 (9): 474–7.

Weaver-Hightower, M. (2003) 'The boy-turn in research on gender and education', *Review of Educational Research*, 73 (4): 471–98.

Wilson, A. (2000) 'There is no escape from third space theory: borderline discourse and the "in between" literacies of prisons', in D. Barton, M. Hamilton and R. Ivanic (eds), *Situated Literacies: Reading and Writing in Context*. London: Routledge. pp. 54–69.

Wohlwend, K. (2009) Early adopters: Playing new literacies and pretending new technologies in print-centric classrooms, *Journal of Early Childhood Literacy*, 9 (2): 117–40.

Wyse, D. and Styles, M. (2007) 'Synthetic phonics and the teaching of reading: the debate surrounding England's "Rose Report"', *Literacy*, 41 (1): 35–42.

Yuill, N., Pearce, D., Kerawalla, C., Harris, A. and Luckin, R. (2009) 'How technology for comprehension training can support conversation towards the joint construction of meaning', *Journal of Research in Reading*, 32 (1): 109–25.

Index

CREATIVE WAYS TO TEACH LITERACY

Ideas for Children aged 3 to 11

Edited by **Virginia Bower**
Canterbury Christ Church University

Covering the essential areas of practice, this book suggests ways to make your literacy teaching as creative and engaging as possible. Children get the most out of their learning when it is exciting, and this book offers great ideas for classroom practice, whilst making careful links to research. Sections advise on teaching narrative, poetry and non-fiction, and each chapter contains case studies and ideas to try out in practice.

The authors cover a broad range of topics, including:

- exploring traditional tales
- writing from experience
- using playground games as a foundation for literacy
- performing poetry.

Written for teachers working with children aged 3-11 years, this book gives you the opportunity to develop children's literacy in enjoyable and interesting ways.

CONTENTS

READERSHIP

Teachers, NQTs and literacy advisers.

June 2011 • 112 pages
Cloth (978-0-85702-045-1) • £60.00
Paper (978-0-85702-046-8) • £19.99

ALSO FROM SAGE